MW01242388

Heart Attacks Happen

Heart

Attacks

Happen

a Memoir on Love & Relationships
Lessons from My Dad, the Men I Loved &
from the Father Above

Ebony Nicole Smith

Copyright © 2022 Ebony Nicole Smith | Heart Attacks Happen

Heart Attacks Happen is a work of non-fiction. Names, places, and incidents have been changed to respect those involved.

All rights reserved. No part of the publication may be reproduced, distributed, or transmitted in any form or by any means, including photocopying, recording, or other electronic or mechanical methods, without the prior written permission of the publisher. Except in the case of a brief quotation embodied in critical reviews and certain other non-commercial uses are permitted by copyright laws.

For permission requests, write to the publisher, addressed "Attention: Permission Coordinator," at the address below.

Published in the United States by Phnixx Vast Publishing, New York.

ISBN: 978-1-7355668-2-5

Book Designed by Ebony Nicole Smith Consulting
Editor: A.B. Brumfield for Omni3Publishing.com

Permission Mailing Address
Ebony Nicole Smith Consulting, LLC
PO BOX 67133
Rochester NY 14617

Other Titles by Author Ebony Nicole Smith

Eve's Confessions: Songs of a Lustful Soul (fiction)

5ive Harts (fiction)

Women Inspiring Nations: Vol 2

Sprinkles of Inspirations

A Praying Wife in Waiting

My Imperfections

Prayers for My Husband (journal)

God Said (journal)

In Pursuit of Fearless Living

Wake Up to Your God-given Purpose

Journaling with Jesus

Dedication

This memoir is dedicated to every woman who is determined to love freely, without the chains or thoughts of the past.

Acknowledgments

As I round out the last few days of year 39, I can't help but think about how far He's brought me. From the deepest valley, He pulled me. Amongst a thick forest, He cleared the way for me. Head barely above water, He threw out a life Savior :-) I can't say I'm where I thought I'd be; however, I can say I'm not where He found me.

I'm thankful for my family, honored to refer to a few as friends, and happy to finally be in love with my God and my Savior. I look forward and up and as year forty creeps in, I'm happier than I've ever been.

My God is setting me up for more than my eyes can see and more than my mind can think. I'm more prepared for whatever He has in store for me.

Dear Woman,

I must admit that I complain to God about things I'm not comfortable complaining to others about. My Pastor preached that we should always, "Complain up instead of down to someone that can't address your complaint." So, one day I was complaining to God when He checked me real hard. He said, "What if for every trouble you had I added a rare gem to your crown and for every complaint you made, I removed two gems? Would you still complain or would you endure the troubles?"

Woman, when I say it put me in my place, sat me down, and caused me to check myself, I mean it. I reflected on my troubles while remembering that He is in control and that all will work out for my good. As a result, I'm sure He's added quite a few gems to my crown. Then, I thought about the gems I lost because of my complaints. Honestly, the last year was complaint after complaint from me to Him. I apologized to God for it all. Yes, He is a shoulder to cry on, but the Scriptures remind me of what God said to Moses at the Red Sea "…Why do you cry to me? Tell the people of Israel to go forward…" (Exodus 14:15 ESV)

Back then, I was stuck in a place I thought I'd never get out of. Instead of moving forward, I cried and complained. #ButGod, being the Father that He is, sent a word to get me moving again. From that, I am once again walking in faith, facing my fears, gripping my Lord's hand, and building confidence in Him and in myself. God is faithful, Woman. Let Him add gems to your crown instead of removing two at a time.

Signed,
Crowned with Gems

Contents

Beautifully Flawed

a Prayer

Lord, we come bearing gifts of praise with our feet, worship in our hands and thanksgiving in our mouths. We hope You accept them.

Lord, forgive us for not seeing ourselves the way You do. Oftentimes, the mirror can be like an enemy to us. We see all the imperfections, those visible to the naked eye and those buried deep within, and we dwell on them. The reflection we see causes us to regret things we did or didn't do while we forget that we were created in the image of the Most High God.

Our waistline has changed over time along with other things that aren't the same as before. We judge ourselves harshly when we look at others. Forgive us for our forgetfulness, for forgetting all the things You've done for us and said to us. From the top of our head to the bottom of our feet, we see things that aren't as we want them to be. But, Lord, if we could only see ourselves the way You do, then we'd see that we are precious, honored, and loved.

If we had Your eyes, we could see that the scars of our past are the beauty marks of our future. If we could see like You do, we'd see our flaws, faults, and failures make us beautifully imperfect, beautifully flawed, and wonderfully made. Lord, help us see, with Your eyes, ourselves.

Help us to change what can be changed and embrace what can't. From the place where our crowns rest to the place of our steps, remind us of how beautiful we are. You've done too much for us not to see that we are created to be Yours in all our flaws.

Amen.

(Isaiah 6:8, Jeremiah 1:5, Isaiah 43:1-7)

1

Ebony Nicole Smith

Section One: Pre-Existing Conditions

A heart attack strikes someone about every 43 seconds. It occurs when the blood flow that brings oxygen to the heart muscle is severely reduced or cut off completely. This happens because the arteries that supply the heart with blood can slowly narrow from a buildup of fat, cholesterol, and other substances (plaque).

Several health conditions, your lifestyle, your age, and your family history can increase your risk for heart disease and heart attack. These are called risk factors. About half of all Americans have at least one of the three key risk factors for heart disease: high blood pressure, high blood cholesterol, and smoking. Some risk factors cannot be controlled, such as your age or family history. But you can take steps to lower your risk by changing the factors that are within control.

How to Tell If You are Experiencing a Heart Attack

A heart attack, also called a myocardial infarction, happens when a part of the heart muscle doesn't get enough blood.

The more time that passes without treatment to restore the blood flow, the greater the damage to the heart muscle.
When it comes to having a heart attack, death is one of the lingering thoughts that keep many from understanding what it can do to one's life.
Will I die from this?
My heart is failing me.
Will the doctors save me?
What will become of my family?
What will the quality of my life be like?
These are a few questions I've thought of as pre and post-questions for someone with a clogged, failing heart. For others, they don't even realize they're having a heart attack, they discount their symptoms as the result of something else altogether. By doing this, they prolong the lifesaving treatment, an intervention that could save their lives.

To effectively express and explain what the *heart attacks* I am referring to felt like, I'll be using medical symptoms to do so.

Sweating
Chest pains and/or discomfort
Shortness of breath, lightheadedness
Fatigue
Pain or discomfort in the arm(s), back, jaw, neck, or stomach
No symptoms
Those were the signs and symptoms that accompanied my *heart attacks*.

One of the boldest things I've ever done in my life was allow God to fix the one part of me that I was too afraid to give away after having given it to those who never deserved it in the first place. My heart. The past can have an effect on the present and hinder the future if it isn't addressed and handled in a proper manner. It was time for me to be healed, and the only way I could start doing that was by learning to deal with my past and the things that had affected, was affecting, and would affect my heart.

One of the ways God taught me to handle the healing of my heart was to acknowledge that there was a problem. For so long I would blame men for my failed relationships. I would also push my lack of relationship with my dad and the emotions that resulted from that onto whomever I was dating. Within weeks of allowing God to repair my heart, I understood that I also had a part in those failures and what my faults were in the failure of those relationships. The understanding wasn't easy to come by because I was so used to being the victim, saying things like, "They all cheated on me." Or, "I loved them all; I don't know why they did me so wrong." Or, "I was a good woman to them. I didn't do anything wrong."

Although I had been cheated on, did love them, and was a good woman to them, my extreme desire for a husband to love me, to give me children, and to spend the rest of his life with me clouded my judgment when it came to being with them. I very distinctly saw the waving red flags in each of those relationships, but I counted them as praise dancers waving flags of worship to a gospel song that only I could hear. But now, having survived the attacks and the surgery, and being out of recovery, I can clearly see where I was a huge part of those relationship failures. Moreso, they weren't the only ones with red flags. If I can be honest, I too had a lot of bright red flags waving in front of them. And just like I ignored theirs, for the most part, they ignored mine. Some even went as far as waving their own flags to match my rhythm.

All that I'll be sharing in this book is not only for you, but also for me to prove to myself that I am truly a conqueror and that everything worked out for my good.

As Two Become One

Without the Father, the Son, and the Holy Spirit, I would be in a place of total loss when it came to love and relationships. I would still have more desire for the man than for the actual marriage. In fact, I was so clueless as to what marriage really was. I thought it was for me to have a man that I liked, not even loved, and for that man to give me the children I wanted.

I didn't care about the marriage itself nor about the building of a family that included more than just the children. I was focused on what I wanted, my needs, and my desires being met. I wanted the children and I knew I needed the husband to get them. From those truths that would be changed when God began to do a good thing in me, I found myself without a view of marriage and relationships. God had done what I call "blank slated me". This refers to Him wiping everything away I believed to be true about love, relationships, and marriage and replacing my former beliefs with His truth.

When the truth of marriage was revealed to me, I realized that I wasn't ready for that truth at all. What He showed me, taught me, and allowed me to experience was far different than what I had assumed it was. Through this process, I learned that I was looking at marriage and relationships through broken, rose-shaded glasses. I saw only what I wanted to see.

In addition to seeing only what I wanted from and in a relationship, I had no one to be an influence that would challenge my belief. There wasn't a woman or man to set me straight on a healthy path to relationships and marriage. This lack only fueled the wrong I thought was so right.

It makes me wonder, as I type this paragraph, how many other women enter into a relationship or better yet, a marriage, with a predetermined understanding of how it works? I wonder how many have it wrong. I would also like to know how many have failed to do the work required to be ready for a relationship or marriage and carried that preparedness into their marriage. I can only guess that it's a lot. I can only guess that many thought they knew what to do as a woman in a relationship only to find that what they knew was nowhere near what was actually required.

I know for me, my idea of marriage was based on one of the most iconic television shows of the late 1980s. The Cosby Show. In real life, you couldn't tell me that within thirty minutes, a family could have an issue, solve it, continue to love each other and keep building a strong family tree. It would be hard-pressed for me not to believe that women and men who were married never fought, belittled each other, cheated, and/or had outside kids. Seeing a father missing from the home wasn't what I saw on television, so I knew, based on that TV show, that my home was broken because of the lack we had.

While watching Tv, I had unknowingly made up my mind that The Cosby Show was how family and marriage should be. For so long it was what I wanted. I wanted the Cliff and Claire Huxtable marriage. I wanted six kids who would go off to college and then off into the world to make my husband and me proud. Then they would come back home with a spouse and children of their own.

I wanted to be an attorney like Claire and hoped my husband would be a doctor like Cliff. That reasoning was why I was so active on the debate team, the pre-trial team, and other groups in high school that were law based. I attended college with the hopes of being like Claire. I was certain I would meet my husband at the University. I was certain that when we met, we would fall in love, follow my agenda, not his, get married, move into some nice area in NY State and live out the best days of our lives together.

I think the reality that I wouldn't become Clair finally hit me when I found myself flunking out of college, miscarrying a baby I didn't know was within me, and ending a two-year relationship because I wasn't happy. That lack of happiness was due to my unexpressed and unrealistic expectations of the man I was with.

My Heart of Hope

My hope is that as you read this book you find yourself relating to my heart and begin to allow God to do a good thing with yours. He said to me, many years ago, "My daughters desire to be wives, but they have not allowed Me to make them a good thing." As you read, judge me and yourself. See that we both have faults, failures, and flaws. Notice how through it all God still chooses us, keeps us, gives us grace and mercy, a purpose, beauty for ashes, and a love that has no boundaries.

Each chapter of this book explains how a series of heart attacks led to the massive attack that would shake, shape, and change my life. If you're not ready for a change of heart, for the surgery needed to get you on the road to recovery, then stop now, close the book, and burn it! This isn't for you. If you'll need to be put to sleep while God works, this isn't for you. If, to you, healing is suppressing emotions, once again, stop reading. This book isn't for you. Accountability is a must. If you dodge it like you would a ball, just close the book and toss it in the trash. Unwilling to allow God to do a good thing in you because of the pain that will come with it? This isn't what you want to read.

My sister, if the easy route to a healthy relationship and a healthy marriage is what you're looking for, I implore you to return this book and get your money back. You will not find what you're looking for within the pages of this book. But what you will find is hope that you can be healed, made whole, and recover from some of life's most trying relationships. What you will obtain is a healthy understanding of marriage and relationships. Being honest with yourself is a huge component of the growth you will experience. No longer will you be able to, or be awarded with, the comfort of lying to yourself about the trauma prior relationships have left on your heart and life. Sitting with yourself and evaluating the matters of your heart will be critical. I know it can be hard, but trust me, I had to do it and the benefits are well worth it. You'll get a much-needed look, and an extensive exploration into the deeper part of you.

> "Search me, O God, and know my heart! Try me and know my thoughts."
> Psa 139: 23 ESV

The psalmist was on to something when he asked the Lord to try him. Essentially, he was telling the Lord to look into the places that others will never or can't see and put the matter of the heart to test. If God were to search your heart, what would He find out? What are the hidden secrets within that the Lord would come to know and possibly reveal to you? Would you be ready for the good work He would do by trying you?

When you allow God to search out the "contents" of your heart, you'll be surprised and stung by what He finds. There may be fragments of toxicity that are so old and worn out that you couldn't imagine them affecting you today. But they can. I call them active pain points. Active pain points are comments or actions that cause a mental, emotional, physical, or even spiritual reaction. It's like hearing something and saying, "Ouch!" to it. Or it's like someone doing something, knowingly or unknowingly, that causes you to move in a defensive way but you're unsure why you moved that way.

The active pain point can show up at just the thought of the situation from yesteryear that caused it. If you've ever felt your heart flutter because of something someone has said, the pain from long ago is still lingering. Those are active pain points.

There are, of course, many other ways an active pain points can be tapped. Sometimes you don't think about it. You may write the sudden emotional discomfort off as the person, the offender as being rude and insensitive to you. But actually, you're still hurt from the first time those words or actions were done to you. That's a cue that you're not as healed as you think. Although, you've moved past it, no longer see the original offender, no longer talk about it or think about it, if you're still reacting to it, it's still there. Your mind is a very powerful tool, causing even your body to react to the memory of those moments.

If you've ever worked out in the gym with a personal trainer, he or she probably explained why it is important to mix up the workout sessions. Because the muscles can become used to doing a certain thing in the gym, you have to "confuse" them to as you work out. Typically, it's switching up the pounds of the weight as you do your reps, or it's doing cardio one day, legs the other day, and arms the following day. You don't want your muscles to remember what it did the day before, so you give them rest then go back to work that part of the body a couple of days later. That is how you build muscles.

As with confusing your muscles, your heart and body react to active pain points the same way. Although you may not consciously remember the full extent of a thing that hurt or traumatized you, the rest of you do. Through time and space, you've taught yourself how to move on to the next exercise to confuse the muscle of your heart. You leave one relationship for the next and you bring the experiences of the prior relationship with you. Those experiences aren't going anywhere. They show up a day or two later and alter everything you do.

When he saw that he had not prevailed against him, he touched the socket of his thigh; so the socket of Jacob's thigh was dislocated while he wrestled with him.
Gen. 32: 25 ESV

How does the memory of yesteryear affect your next relationship?

Let's think about it for a minute.

Have you ever said to the new man, "You act just like him?" He may not know, at the moment, whom you're referring to, but you do. Better yet, telling your friends who know all too well what the last one did, you make the comment, "Girl, he acts just like (insert the name). All men are the same."

If you've said anything remotely close to those statements, you still remember, and your heart and body are reacting. Now, could the new lover have done or said something like the one in the past? Sure, but does that mean they are the same? Absolutely not. What happens is that a similar action or statement from your past is given and you respond the same way you did back then. Because your response is the same, the cause of your reaction appears the same.

Let's say that in the prior relationship, you were used to him coming home late, but not from work. Arguments ensued all night with you two fighting verbally or even physically. As you fell asleep in different rooms, you lay there, your mind racing with thoughts of where he was and who he was with. At some later time it was revealed that there was another woman he'd been seeing. So now that you're with someone new, if he comes home late, you automatically think the worst. You respond like before because experience has taught you that the only reason he would stay out late is because he's cheating. Yet, the new man is different. He was with friends just as he said he would be.

"You're lying. You're seeing someone else. Show me proof you were with your friends." How damaging is this to your relationship? There's only but so much one person can take before they reach their breaking point. You're healing is clearly needed. The active pain points and heart muscles are being strained.

Are you tired yet?

I know I was.

The Tree of Bitterness

Alright, let me give you a little insight into the good thing God did in me. I wasn't prepared for the work He did, but I needed it like flowers need the rain. I was in a comfortable space, one I was determined to stay in forever! I felt at home in frustration, loneliness, doubt, man-hating, damaging thoughts, and actions. I was well to think I could be in those places and serve God wholeheartedly. The funny thing is, He couldn't accept my heart the way it was.

The transformation of my heart couldn't have occurred with my own might, I knew this. The more I tried to fix me on my own, the more I hurt myself. That task was more than I could handle alone. Finally, I gave up and God stepped in at the exact point of my failure.

In 2018, November to be exact, a week after my birthday God declared, "I cannot handle a bitter heart. I Am going to remove everything that caused this." My heart had become bitter and useless to both me and God. Years of failed relationships, broken promises, and bad decisions I'd both made and allowed led me to a place of surrendering.

When I threw up my hands and said, "Okay. I'm done," it was the moment I'd stopped running from the memories and allowed God to heal what was badly broken and damaged.

I will go deeper into this later, but for now, I want you to have your time with the Surgeon. I want Him to work on you as He did me. Maybe you don't require as much work on your heart as I did. My operation lasted one and half years, recovery was about another year. It was worth it to endure it all. Who I am today is nothing short of an amazing display of God's miraculous love for me.

He healeth the broken in heart, and bindeth up their wounds.
Psa 147:3 ESV

Are you ready, I mean really ready for this journey toward being healed? I believe that as I reveal the matters of my heart, those situations that caused me to have mini heart attacks that led to the massive one in 2017, you'll be encouraged to seek the help you need to make sure you don't have one as I did.
If you're ready, then so am I.
Heart Attacks Happen, but you too can survive them.
Live.
Love.
Laugh.
And have a bountiful relationship with the Lord.

Sweating

If at any point you begin to sweat profusely, without doing anything to cause your body temperature to rise, you could be having a heart attack.

In life we have moments that change us, moments that pivot us in a direction we never asked to head in, and it becomes the turning point that we will always remember. For me, three moments changed my life and became the pre-existing conditions that led to my repeated heart attacks.

The journey of living with those conditions made the massive attack more important. It was those times that led to a few addictions, bad then worse decisions, and years of low self-esteem.

As a follower of Jesus, I am aware of the impact that releasing my story can have on those who are watching and waiting for me to fail. Yet, since I am writing and living for God, nothing is a failure. All is a lesson learned and a teachable moment.

Here is me having a learned during teachable moment...

The Temperature of the Body Rapidly Rises

I remember the first time my heart was broken. I was roughly seven years old and a trip to the amusement park with my father was my focus. He said he was going to come get my sister and me. Being that he was our dad, we had no reason not to trust him.

A week before the big day, our dad came over to our home in his long, yellow Cadillac. He was just as excited to see us just as we were to see him. We tried to jump into his arms as he walked to the front porch. Giving us pieces of candy, he inquired about how we were doing. We eagerly told him about our day. Then, I added, "Can we go to Seabreeze?" I tugged at the collar of his shirt, hoping he would notice how much I really wanted to go.

Seabreeze was the place where kids could be kids and adults could be…adults with kids. We had not been there all summer and as summer was coming to an end, we wanted to be able to say, when school restarted, that we, too had gone there. Looking down at the faces of his two daughters, our dad said, "Yea, I'll take y'all to Seabreeze next weekend." We jumped up and down with excitement.

At that time, we lived upstairs in the back of a two-family home. I ran up the steps to tell my mom what my dad had said. She said, "Oh. Okay." She asked if he was still there and I happily said that he was. Together, she and I went back outside just as he was entering his car. Mom walked to his car door, "You're taking them to Seabreeze next week?"

Before responding, he got in the car, turned it on, and answered.

"Yea. I'll take them. I'll get my son too."

We had a big brother from another mother. We used to be together a lot as kids, so it was even more exciting to know that he was going with us.

"Okay. What do you want me to do, Lindsay?" Mom asked.

"Just make sure they're ready at noon."

"Okay," she replied and walked away, leaving us at the side of the car.

My dad watched her walk toward the back of the house where we had just come from. Then he told us that he was leaving and leaned over to kiss us. We both held on to the car door, stood on our tippy-toes and kissed our father. His final words to us were, "Be good or your mama not gone let you go."

"We'll be good," was our promise and we did everything we could to keep that promise that whole week.
He instructed us to get back on the sidewalk so he could leave. Doing what our father said, we backed up a safe distance from the road and watched him pull off. We waved and yelled, "I love you," to which he replied the same.

For the longest time we stood there, two hope-filled girls, excited that we were going to Seabreeze with our dad and big brother. We were happy as could be for a promise made to us by the first man to ever love us, our father.

For me, my heart was pumping with joy. All week I did what my mama said. When she told me to go bathe, eat my food, clean my room, watch my sister, go to the store, I did it all without any kickback or complaining. I didn't want her to tell me that I couldn't go with my dad that weekend because I'd been bad. I remember telling our cousins and friends about going to the amusement park that weekend. Everyone was excited for us and wished they were going, too.

"Are you going to get on the Jack Rabbit, Ebony?" My cousin Toya asked me as were sitting on the front porch at my house.

"Yup. I'm going to get on it a lot of times." To be honest, rollercoasters scared the heck out of me. I would get on them one time, but that would be it. Besides that, only being seven years old, I wasn't tall enough for the Jack Rabbit, only for the Bunny Rabbit. The Bunny Rabbit was a very much smaller redemption of the Jack Rabbit. It has a few low rolling hills but didn't go as fast as the bigger one. It was not as extreme, but it scared me, nonetheless.

The day before we were to spend the day with our dad, our mom helped us pick out outfits to wear. I remember picking out a purple windbreaker short set and my sister picked a pair of pink shorts with a white top. I distinctly remember because my mom told her, Don't to get anything on that white shirt because it'll be hard to get the stains out."

After bathing and eating dinner and playing with my Barbie dolls, it was time to go to sleep. I hopped in bed, tossed the cover over my body, and quickly went to sleep. I was sure that the faster I went to sleep, the sooner the morning would come so we could leave.

The next morning came just as quickly as I had hoped. Me and my sister were ready to go with our dad way before the time he'd told our mom to have us ready. We ate a breakfast of Kix cereal and then our mom did our hair. She put my hair into two plaits and my sister's hair into ponytails. We got dressed and waited for twelve p.m. to arrive.

I remember watching the clock for the best time of the day and when it hit, all the pent up excitement came spilling out of us. We grabbed our bookbags, which had a few snacks, our bathing suits, and a towel, then dashed out the back door. I don't know how long it had taken me to get outside to wait on our front porch, but I'm sure I would have beaten Flash up there.

The day was sunny and warm. Nothing was going to stop us from having one of the best days of the summer. We were ready to spend the day with our dad and big brother. I know I wanted to get on every ride there, eat a fried waffle covered in powdered sugar and a hotdog. That was what I and my sister talked about the day before. But that day we sat on the front porch, played in the front yard, and waited. The wait seemed like forever, but we knew it would be worth it.

Eventually our cousins and friends came over to play with us before we left. Running around the neighborhood was not an option because we did not want to miss our dad by having him wait for us to come back. My mom had given us a few dollars and the temptation to spend it at the store when our friends went was real, but we didn't move from in front of the house at all.

We were so strategic about being ready and available when he came that we would take turns going to the bathroom or for water. We never went in the house at the same time because we didn't want him to think we weren't home. We didn't have a car so the lack of one being there wouldn't have been a sign of whether we were home or not. Every time we heard a car coming up the street, we would be right on the sidewalk looking to see it was him, but it was not.

As the day lingered on, our excitement began to slowly go away. My mom came outside a few times to check on us. "He ain't come yet?" We would shake our heads no, but were still filled with hope that he was coming. "Okay," she'd say, then go back into the house.

Looking back on that day, I realize that she'd known the day before that he wasn't coming. She'd known he was lying to us, but she still played along with his lie to keep us from the disappointment that was sure to come.

Our friends kept us company as much as they could, but being kids, they understood that the neighborhood was a playground when our front yard really was not. Soon, the summer sky began to lose its light. As it did, so did I.

My mom, once the sun was gone and the moon had taken its rightful place with the stars, came back outside one last time. "Y'all, come on in the house. He not coming."

I remember her picking up our bookbags, grabbing my little sister's hand, and ushering us inside. We began to cry as we ascended the stairs to our apartment. With each step I took, the heavier my heart became. Nothing from the week prior had prepared me for that letdown. I'd been braced for a fun-filled day, but instead I was filled with sorrow and the biggest let-down of my young life.

Mom made dinner for us that night after telling us to change our clothes and empty out our bookbags. Doing as she said, my sister and I moved in silence while our tears dropped down our faces. I don't know what she was thinking but I was thinking that he didn't come because of something I had done. There had to be a reason for him not showing up and since my young mind couldn't think of anything else, I had to be the reason. I wondered if I should have called my grandma to get in contact with him. I replayed the idea of going to my uncle's house to see if he knew where our dad was.

I wished I had searched for him to remind him of what he'd said, but I couldn't change the past. I was stuck in the present. The future wasn't a thought. I just couldn't understand why he hadn't shown up. With extreme sadness hovering over me like a black cloud, all I wanted to do was sleep because I didn't know what else to do. As I tried to rest, I was still hopeful that he would come later that night, but my hope was pointless. At that age, I'd learned how to have hope in a hopeless situation.

It was the first time my heart had ever been broken. It was the first time me and my sister cried for our dad together. It was the first time I cried myself to sleep and was the first time I thought that I was the reason why a man did not keep a promise made to me.

It was the first time for a lot of hurts, but sadly, it would not be the last.

He heals the brokenhearted and binds up their wounds.
Psa 147:3 ESV

My Dad. My First Love. My First Heart Attack!

A father can never know the depths of his daughter's heart unless it is he that takes her to that place of heartache, loneliness, and longing. She'll try, with her words, to express herself, but if his heart isn't open to hers, he'll never understand. For so long I tried to tell my father how much I loved and hated him at the same time, but my words fell on a closed heart and deaf ears. He didn't know that he'd set the tone for how I perceived and received men.

Despite how my father treated us, I still wanted him to be my dad, still wanted to make him proud, still wanted to hear him say, "Daughter, I'm proud of you." I wanted the relationship little girls on television had with their fathers. The Cosby Show was the family life I wanted. I daydreamed about a "Cliff and Rudy" type of relationship with my dad. I wanted to sit and talk over ice cream, play in the park, have tea parties, and just be father and daughter.

All I'd gone through would stay with me well into adulthood and it shaped my relationship with men. Everything that had gone wrong in my relationships, I thought was my fault. I wanted the relationships written for television. The ones where the man loved the woman and took care of her. I wanted the man who was the hopeless romantic, the defender of his family but I was the issue that ruined us.

It was during my 33rd year of life that God said to me, "Let Me Be Who I Am." I wasn't sure what He meant by that but as I questioned for understanding, He gave me what I needed. He wanted me to let Him be the Father I needed. He wanted me to let Him cover me not just as God but as a Father covers his daughter. I needed a father and allowed Him to be what I needed.

Through His love and care for me, He showed me how a father is supposed to care for his daughter. He made me confront the pain and despair left in my heart from years of trauma caused by the lies of my father and the men I chose to date. I had to revisit those years and moments through meditation, prayer, and writing. I allowed the bitterness to flow from my heart by realizing that I controlled what affected it. Allowing God to be the Father I desired caused me to no longer seek my father to be such.

Since my dad has passed away, I can't tell him how I felt for so long. There's no way for me to search for him so he could know that I wanted a relationship with him. Staying stuck in the past wasn't an option. I had to literally let go and let God handle the matters of my heart. When I did, everything began to change. If I could tell my dad anything it would be:

Dear Dad,

Thank you for being the first man that I loved. Thank you for showing me, though I wasn't aware at the time, how a man is to be vetted as an option. Thank you for showing me that a man should always have his own and that he shouldn't rely on me to have his basic needs met. Thank you for loving me in the capacity at which you knew how. Thank you for the memory that makes me smile, even now.

I remember when I was turning ten years old and you promised me that you would bring me a gift for my birthday. I had no idea what it would be but that didn't stop me from guessing. My mind went everywhere it wanted in guessing what gift you would bring me. When my birthday arrived I was even more excited about it. It would have been the first time in a long time that you had given me a gift. I knew that whatever it was, it had to be good. Coming home from school, I remember sitting in the living room within view of the front picture window. I kept looking out for you. Every car that went by, I was hoping it was you but it wasn't. I had become a bit saddened because the day turned into night and brought with it rain.

The rainfall was cold and fast. I gave up thinking you would come to me in bad weather at night. I remember going to my room and crying alone because I felt my birthday was over. Later in the evening, my mom called out my name. She told me someone was at the door for me. Rushing out of my room, down the hallway, and onto the porch I found you at the door, standing in the rain on a cold November night holding a pizza box.

My mom didn't allow you to come into our home, so there you stood. I remember your face lighting up when you saw me and mine doing the same. You wished me, "Happy birthday," and handed me the box. I have to admit, I wasn't all that happy with a pizza because my mom had already cooked dinner. However, I was happy to see you and thankful for the pizza box. You said to me, "Open it." I guess you could see the disappointment on my face. You were kind enough to hold the box while I opened it. And when I did, to my surprise, it was a homemade chocolate cookie cake that you made just for me! I smiled and giggled at the sight of seeing 'Happy Birthday, Ebony' written in purple frosting.

"Thank you!" I yelled as we both held the box so I could wrap an arm around your neck, and you wrapped your arm around my waist. You kissed me and said, "I love you, baby girl."
Allowing this gapped toothed smile to take over my face, I happily replied, "I love you too, Dad."

You told me that you had to work at the school first and then, after getting permission to use the school's ovens, you had to bake the cookie cake for me. That's why you were late coming over. You had to work and then prepare the gift for me. I understand now. And I appreciate that cookie cake even more.

It was cold that November 14th. But that didn't stop you from standing in the rain to see your baby girl's face as she opened the pizza box with the homemade chocolate cookie cake in it. The rain didn't matter as you stood watching me show the gift to my little sister and our mom. It didn't matter that you were drenched from head to toe. That didn't matter because what did matter to you...was me and the promise you made to bring me a gift like you said you would.

I wonder if you remembered the promise of Seabreeze that one summer which you didn't want to repeat. I wonder if you thought about how you let me and Meka down then and didn't want to do it again. I wonder if you knew I was waiting all day for you, filled with hope and high expectations. I wonder if you knew I would wait as long as I had to, to see the gift you had for me on my birthday. I wonder.
However, all is well with my soul, Dad. All is well. I get it now. I really do get it. You went through the whole day knowing you were going to do what you said. While I went through the day wondering what it was and if you were really going to come over with what you said you had for me.

While we both had different experiences that day, we both had the same goal: to see each other smile from the gift that was given. Dad, thank you for standing in the rain for me.
Thank you for standing in the rain for me.
Thank you for standing in the rain for me.
Signed,

I get it now and will forever.

What I understand now is that my dad had a plan for me. What I had no idea of was how he was going to do it or what that gift was. I just knew there was a gift coming on a specific day for a specific reason. He had to get permission to bake the cookie cake on the school grounds, using their equipment during after-hours. He was a janitor for a local high school, I understand now that he had to do some things that I wasn't aware of to accomplish what he'd promised me. I understand now that he did what was needed, standing in the rain, to see me on the day he said. Even though he wasn't allowed in our home, he waited in the rain…for me.

What my dad did for me then is what God is doing for me even now and forever. Everything He promised me, He is working and preparing. Even when it rains in my life, He is standing there waiting for me to come to the door that has been opened just for me. He is waiting for me to arrive to open the gift He made just for me. He is waiting at the door, holding a gift that, at first glance, wasn't how I thought it would or should arrive. I'm learning that even God gives gifts that don't look the way we want them to look and that don't come wrapped in packages we would normally accept. But what's inside those packages is more than we could ask or think of. He is our greatest Gift waiting to be opened. His love, care, and kindness are gifts.

Side Effects

Is This What Love Is?

That first heartbreak was the fertile ground in which a small seed called bitterness had been planted. Of course, with my lack of understanding emotions, I didn't know that what I felt, what I had carried with me all those years, was bitterness. Sadly, the ground that had been stirred up was ripe for the filling of anything and everything designed to destroy me.

In the early '90's, kids had no worries in the world; well, at least the kids I grew up with. We weren't rich but we weren't poor, again from what I saw. Having fun being kids was all we had to do. Keeping up with each other as we ran around the neighborhood was a "worry" we had. Learning how to ride a bike without falling and getting hurt was another. Other than that, we were good. So, I had no idea about or interest in liking anyone or anyone liking me. Therefore, it was total surprise to find that I had a boy liking me.

One day, while we were all playing outside my aunt's house, I was told, "I like you," by the thirteen year old grandson of my aunt's neighbor.

At eight years old, I had never heard of a boy liking me and was surprised because I didn't feel, and hadn't been told, I was cute. I was a chubby kid with very short hair which was such because my grandmother had given me a hair relaxer one week and then two-weeks later had given me a Jheri curl. As a result, I'd lost all of my hair. I didn't feel cute or likable.

This boy was no stranger to me, he was a teenager I'd seen for years since my family and his family had grown up together. He, my cousins and sisters, and the other neighborhood kids all played together. Running up and down the streets, playing with jump rope, hide-n-seek, riding bikes and doing what kids do. I didn't know that at eight years old I had garnered the attention of that boy, my focus at that time was on running from my cousin who would chase me with ants. But I do remember how he and I ended up in a dark garage one night.

A large group of us were playing hide-n-seek when I ran into the garage to hide before making my way to base. Peeking out from behind a box, I saw him hurry in. He hid behind an old junk car and when he saw me, he waved me over to him. Staying low, I moved to the back of the car with him. "Get down," he instructed me so we wouldn't be found. We were crouched over, hiding from the enemy that was chasing everyone, and before I knew it, he was kissing me.

I froze, absolutely unsure of what to do, when he stuck his cold tongue in my mouth and moaned. Quickly, I pulled back to stare at him, I was confused about what he was doing and why. He told me not to worry, said he was just playing a game with me. Then he told me not to tell anyone and asked if I wanted him to get into trouble. I shook my head no because he was my friend. I knew his grandma was not a joke and that she would have broken his neck for kissing me. Not only that, but my mama would also have kicked my tail for letting a boy kiss on me. I was afraid of what my mom would do to me, so I agreed not to tell a soul.

He stared at me in the dark and for a moment, looking back now, I could see that he wanted to do other things, to take that kiss much farther, but the yells of, "Base!" from the other kids who made it to the front porch of another neighbor's house stopped him. Suddenly, he jumped up and ran toward that base and I followed. I barely made it to safety. I do not know who was "it" after that, but it was definitely not me.

Restarting the game, everyone had taken off running again as the seeker began to loudly count to fifty. We scattered like roaches trying to find a place to hide during that summer night when the moon was high and the adults were inside, just as high as the moon, listening to music, drinking, and playing Spades. "Hide with me again," the teenager said as he grabbed my hand and we ran together back to the dark garage that was slightly lit by the glowing shine of the moon.

Once inside, he led me to the back of the car again and there, he did not kiss me on my lips as he had that first time. Instead, his fingers moved to a place that should not have been touched, at least until marriage or until I was old enough to make the decision myself.

Things moved quickly in the span of time we were hidden behind that old rusty car. He would give me instructions that changed my life and stole the innocence that was in me. The time it had taken him to become a thief and me a victim was long enough for me to bleed and feel a burning sensation down below. I remember crying out, but he covered my mouth and told me to shut up before he got in trouble. So, I did.

I was changed. I was different. I was silenced. I was hurt. I was stolen.

The smell of the car motor oil bothered me and the smell of gasoline did too. The cold ground chilled my warm skin from the bottom while the heaviness of his body warmed me from the top. I felt like my body no longer belonged to me, and the ground, which I used to sit on with my friends to draw using chalk, let me down. It was the ground that kept me from moving from beneath him. I had nowhere to go. I was stuck.

To escape, I closed my eyes and in my mind I went to a place of safety: my bedroom. My room was the place I could go when I wanted to be alone, to play by myself, and to get rest from the day. I felt like home was the place where nothing bad could happen to me because there I was loved and cared for by my mom. Home was where my life was secure and nothing could get to me. Home was where I went as I lay on the concrete while the most sacred part of me was being ravaged.

The sound of winners reaching base, cheering other hiders to come out or run faster to get away from the seeker began to trickle into the dark space. But those sounds were nowhere near as loud as he was in my ear. His groans would tingle my ears for years to come. Then, just as quickly as it had begun, it was over. He left a part of himself inside of me that night and that would be carried there just as his moaning and groaning would be carried in my memory.

Finally, we emerged from the darkness and went our separate ways. He entered the back door of his grandma's house and disappeared. I stood next to a bush and cried. My mind couldn't explain to itself what happened, so I knew I wouldn't be able to explain it to anyone else. I "fixed my face," because I didn't want any of the kids or my mom to ask me why I was crying. I used my shirt to wipe away my tears and tried not to focus on the wetness between my legs.

Instead of going to 'base' where the other kids were standing, waiting for all the other kids to make it or for one to get caught, I made my way into my aunt's house.

I heard someone yell out, "Where you goin'?" It was one of the adults.

I replied, "I have to pee," which was not a lie. I did have to pee.

In the bathroom, I pulled my pants down and covered my mouth to keep from verbally expressing my pain. There was a thick substance in my panties that I had never seen before. I didn't know what it was and I didn't want it there, so I used a bunch of tissue to clean my panties and myself. As I urinated, I felt a burning down below. I wanted to yell from the pain of that but I didn't. I simply finished peeing, then I gently wiped myself so as not to cause any more pain down there.

As I was cleaning up all evidence of the worst moment of my life, there was a knock at the bathroom door and someone yelling at me to, "Hurry up because other people need to use the bathroom!" In a state of complete shock from what had taken place, I acknowledged the request and did what was asked.

I didn't know what I was going to do once I went back outside, I was afraid but knew I couldn't just hide in the house, sitting with the adults. They would have sent me back into the darkness with the famous, "Get outta grown folks' business." The only choice I had was to venture back to the place I didn't want to go again. The dark. Standing at the side door, I looked out at the street, trying to gauge whether or not I could see him. I wanted to avoid him at all costs. As it turned out, I couldn't because like a sore thumb, he stuck out. He was laughing with some of the other boys while eating something. He appeared to have forgotten what he had done. Smiling and enjoying the night air was his pleasure, but not mine.

My heart raced and I began to breathe heavily. I felt dizzy and wanted to run back into the house, but I could not because I was not grown enough to be around the adults. I felt tears swell up, immediately ready to fall. I fought hard to hold them back. Had I allowed them to trickle down my face, I would've had to explain why I was crying. The sad thing was that I didn't know the words to express or explain my tears.

What could I have said, "He hurt me,"? Had I given that explanation, I'm sure the follow-up question would have been, "What did he do?" I knew what'd happened, I just didn't have the words in my vocabulary to verbalize the answer to that question. So, I held back my tears and didn't say anything. Looking back, I wish I would've used the limited words I did have to tell the world.

Since I didn't have an out, I gripped the porch's handrail and descended the four steps to the pathway that led to the front of the house. Everything in me wanted to sit on the steps until it was time to go home. I wanted to sink into the concrete of the steps until I heard my mom call for me and my sister to come to her. But those were not options I could take. As I headed down the path to the front porch, my cousin was running toward me.

She asked innocently, "Where were you?" and followed that up with "Everyone was ready to play again."
Play again.
Play again.
Play again.

I didn't want to play again. The first time I "played", my soul was snatched from me and I was tossed into a place of solitude and silence. But I kept my mouth shut and followed her to the street where the rest of our friends were. They were standing by a car ready to play hide-n-seek once again. For me, however, I wasn't going to do it. Instead, I stood on the sidewalk and watched them play in the darkness. That game was no longer a time of fun in my world, it was a time of horror, mistreatment, and fear.

When the night came to an end, I was happy to walk around the corner with my mom and sister to go home. I was happy to get off that street and away from him.

The thoughts I had that evening were all over the place.

"What if my mama finds out?"

"I'm going to get in trouble if I say something."

"I don't like the dark."

Reaching home, my safe place, I went to my room and sat on the floor next to my bed. I didn't cry because I still didn't want to explain why I was crying. I smelled my shirt and my hands; they smelled like gasoline. I turned up my nose and quickly removed the shirt. I grabbed my nightshirt, slipped that on, then returned to the floor.

Sitting there, I replayed the night's event. I thought about ways I could have avoided him. I came up with ways to dodge him and run out of the garage the first time. Then there was the action of snatching my hand away from him so I wouldn't end up in the dark with him again. I saw myself telling my mom what he'd done and saw her hugging me and then going next door to tell his grandma. I saw the police coming to take him away and his little brothers crying at the sight of it. I envisioned him being put away for a long time to keep other girls safe.

If I had told, other girls would be safe and no one would ever be hurt again. But that was not my reality. So, my imagination became the second place of safety for me. It hid the truth by covering it with a different perspective. If I were able to think of something different than what happened, then those thoughts would become what really happened and I wouldn't be sad or afraid any longer.

"I say to you, My friends, do not be afraid of those who kill the body and after that have nothing more that they can do."

Luke 12:4

Breathing In to Let It All Out

My sister came in and told me that I had to take a bath. Getting up from the floor, I undressed again. When I pulled my panties down for the second time after what had happened, I saw that there was a lingering stain in the crotch area. I had to quickly think of what to do with my underwear so my mom wouldn't find them. I searched and searched around my room until I found a brown paper bag that I'd gotten from going to the corner store at some other time. I balled my panties up and placed them in the bag, then balled it up. Needing a place to hide it until I could put it in the trash, I stuck it the bag and its contents in a corner behind a stuffed animal.

Secure that no one would find my secret, I grabbed my towel, wrapped it around my body, headed to the bathroom, and got into the tub. As I lowered myself into the warm water, the burning sensation caused me to stand up quickly. I put my hand over it and cried. The soreness hurt to the point where I didn't want to wash up and I didn't. I know it sounds crazy to have not cleansed that area, but I didn't want to because what hurt would only hurt more. Instead, I used the washcloth to wipe myself down everywhere but there.

I scrubbed my arms and hands extra to get the smell of the gasoline off my skin. I don't remember how many times I did it, but it felt like it took forever to get rid of that smell. The odor could have been gone the first time, but I kept smelling it, it kept tormenting me, so I kept washing it away. I didn't want that smell on me because I had quickly grown to despise it. Even to this day, I hate the smell of motor oil and gasoline.

After I was finished, I wrapped myself in a towel and headed back to my room where I would lie in bed and cry myself to sleep. I went to bed without eating that night, I had absolutely no appetite to do so. For some reason, crying about the thievery that had occurred made me think of my dad. My young mind decided that if he'd been there, that would never have happened. He would have beaten him up for touching his baby girl and hurting her. Again, my imagination showed me a different perspective on the truth. In that perspective, my dad was the hero that saved me from the bad boy next door.

My dad was my missing hero. I was waiting for him to come and save me but he never arrived just as he hadn't shown up when he'd promised to take us to the amusement park. I wondered if that was love, if making promises and not being there for your daughter was what love was. There was no one to teach me otherwise because I had not a way to ask it without confusing myself. I would have been confused because my dad said he loved me, but sometimes didn't act like it. It didn't seem like he loved me at all because he was always missing. Twenty-something years had passed before I finally learned the truth about love and about what it was.

To be clear, I hid the evidence of what happened, kept a lock on the words that could have set me free, and never shared the darkness that was around me with my mom because I didn't know how to tell her any of it. I know, you may think, "You could have told someone." You're right, I could have. But the words just would not come out of my mouth. My mom loved us and protected us the best she could. Like many kids, we didn't know what we could or couldn't get in trouble for doing or not doing.

As a result, I thought what happened was my fault and that I would get a whipping for not saying something the first time. I should have, could have, told my mom that he had kissed me in the dark, but being eight years old, I thought it would have been my fault because I was in the dark with a boy, which was a no-no.

I didn't share it then, but I share this now because I don't want anyone to think my mom was a bad mother. She wasn't. I chose not to tell her because of my own fears. I couldn't tell her because I didn't know how to. I would have told her but the voice that told me to, "Shut up," kept ringing in my ears along with the sound of his pleasure.

Some people believe that a parent or guardian should be aware of what is happening to their child. I can agree to an extent. But if something has happened or is happening and the child does not or cannot say what it is, how can the parent know? I have never once faulted my mother for what happened to me, she wasn't there. She had no idea. I wish I would have said something the first time, however, I can't change the past so there's no need to linger where change is not possible.

It was on that night that I began to fear the dark. Since then, I was never able to sleep in the pitch black. I would sleep with the closet door open and with the light on. When I became an adult, I slept with a light on somewhere in the room because of that fear of the dark.

"I create the light and make the darkness. I send good times and bad times. I, the LORD, am the one who does these things..." Isa. 45:7 NLT.

Speak in Silence

Remembering such a painful moment in my life's journey wasn't easy. The task of opening an old, healed, uninfected wound was hard. However, as He (God) has reminded me many times, "Your story is for My glory" and that is what keeps me bleeding out to help someone else heal.

Isn't that what Jesus did for us? (Isaiah 53:5 ESV)

What keeps us from doing the same for someone else?
The things that happened to me and what I had to do to cover them up was surely going to go with me to my grave. There was no way in this world I was going to release those actions from my lips. I was confident that my silent pain was protected with smiles and an eagerness to help and protect others. As long as I did those things, no one would ever know, right?
Wrong.

I think it was my younger cousin that eventually "ratted" me out to my mother, but one thing for sure is that everyone knew what happened.

On another evening like the first, we were all playing again. Once more, he pulled me back behind that rusted, oil-smelling car and began to fondle me. He didn't get a chance to insert anything anywhere that time because my cousin "caught" us. Or should I say, she saved me.
The moment I realized my cousin knew, I ran after her, begging her not to tell on me. I cried from fear of being beaten. Storming the house until she found her audience, my cousin told my mom what she'd caught me doing. I can't recall what my mom said or did, I just know she never gave me that beating. I do remember sitting at the kitchen table in his grandma's house listening to the adults talk about what happened.

As much as I wish I could give details of the night, I can't. It's all spotty and foggy. The parts I do remember involved my telling of only the incident my cousin had seen. I never told them about the other times. I didn't tell them that he had done much worse to me. I was too afraid to tell them, I was afraid of him, and I didn't want to speak of the incident then or before.

The strange thing was that no one ever asked me what happened. As a result, I didn't talk about it and silence became another place of safety for me. If I don't speak about it, it didn't happen. If it didn't happen, I can't be affected. If I'm not affected...well, there's no way to escape the infection that comes with the effect of what I chose not to speak about. Silly me thinking not speaking would cancel everything out. The truth is that what I was doing or not doing only caused me to learn not to speak when things bothered me. It taught me that my emotions weren't valid. It taught me how to effectively muzzle my voice. Like a dog, the only thing I could do was growl in pain but no one knew such pain existed in me.

Looking back, I realize that I was more afraid of being beaten for not saying anything sooner. It wasn't, as I explained before, a fear my mom put in me. It was just a fear that I conjured up and that fear kept me quiet. I guess back then there wasn't such a thing as "a safe space" for kids. Had there been, I probably would have felt safe enough to tell the adults what transpired when it first happened.

My hope now is that I am able to create a safe space for my nephews and nieces, and one day my own children, to come and talk to me about things that happen to them and that trouble them.

The Cool Down

Life is funny at times and many of those times I don't even remember.

From the age of nine until the age of twelve, there are missing spans of time that I have not been able to recover. With the writing of this book, I was hoping that my memory would somehow be jogged, and a recollection of those experiences would come in like a raging flood. But no, it has not. I honestly have no remembrance of what life was like back then except for my 10th birthday and the death of my grandma, my father's mother.

I remember coming home one day from where I do not recall and having my stepdad tell me that my mom was around the corner at my uncle's house. He told me that my grandma, Marylou, had passed away. I don't remember how old I was, but I do recall walking around the corner to my uncle's house and seeing my mom and dad walking up the street as they saw me coming. I began to cry as I reached them and they both hugged me. I followed them to the house where all my family were. From there, I only remember the day of her funeral. We were in the procession line heading to the burial site. Out of the blue a car cut my mom off, breaking into the line of grieving family members. I don't know exactly what I said, but I remember swearing and my mom saying that it was okay.

From there everything was blank. Foggy. Spotty.

The next thing I can recall is the day the door to destruction and a life filled with addiction was kicked in.

At the age of eleven I had a best friend named Ebony. No, not myself, but an actual friend named Ebony. She was big Ebony because she was taller than me and I was just Ebony. Where and when you saw her you saw me and vice versa. We were thick as thieves she and I. During our friendship, she had become pregnant at just eleven years old. I was told by my mom that my best friend was having a baby. For some reason, still a mystery to me, I sat on the steps that led to my bedroom in the attic and cried. I cried as if it were me.

Gathering myself after a while, I went outside, crossed the street to her home and talked to her. I found out that she'd been having sex with her stepbrother who was sixteen years old. I don't know if it was forced or not, but I knew she was a child and all that she could agree to was being such and nothing more. We still played as we'd done before, but as her belly grew, so did my curiosity of how it felt to have a baby growing inside of her. She would show me her belly as the baby rolled around, watching it made me want to feel what she was feeling, it made me want to be pregnant too. Looking back, I now understand that it was more about the attention she was getting from others that made me want to have a baby. I don't know, I just wanted what she was having. It wouldn't be too long before I 36ouldd have what she had, But it wasn't the fanfare I assumed it would be.

Being that I was an inquisitive little girl, it was strange to me that I noticed everything except when something was off about a situation or person. By the time I noticed, it would be far too late. That's how it was with the next series of events that took place in my life. I noticed everything too late.

I remember the first day I saw him. He was a tall, chubby, older boy that lived next door to me. I liked him because he was able to come and go as he pleased and because he was funny and cute. At seventeen years old, there were not many rules that his parents applied to him and I liked that. A lot.

Although I was paying attention to him, he didn't notice me, or so I thought. Every time he came home and I saw him, I would blush when he arrived. He would just look and say, "Hey," to everyone that was around, then he would go inside for a while, come back out, and leave again. I don't know why I liked that so much, but I did. Needless to say, he didn't pay me any attention, but I gave him all the attention I had, which was limitless in my imagination.

One day, my next-door neighbor, whose name I cannot remember, befriended me and Ebony. She was one of ten kids, I believe she was the fourth oldest child. We all hung out that summer and grew to become a female version of The Three Musketeers. As the summer moved on, we did less running around and more sitting because of the growth of Ebony's belly. While hanging on that particular neighbor's front porch, she decided that she wanted to have a sleepover with the three of us. Ebony and I asked our mothers and they agreed. Her brother wasn't home when we finally went in once it had become late, he didn't arrive until later that evening and he was with his best friend at that time.

Listen, when I say I have a spotty memory about some stuff, trust that I do. I don't know how it all happened, but I remember my best friend being in his room with both him and his best friend. I was in his sister's room with her when a condom came flying through her open bedroom door followed by my best friend. She picked the condom up and told me that he'd heard I liked him. From there, I found myself in his room sitting on his bed.

When I first got into the room, I saw that the three of them were watching pornography. As a woman was giving a man oral sex on the screen, he said to me, "You ever done that?" I shook my head no and he said, "You should try it." Then I looked down and there, on the floor of his room, my best friend and his best friend were having sex. I told him I didn't want to do that, to which he replied, "Okay." The next thing I knew, he was feeling on my breasts and kissing me. He told me, "Relax," as my body had tensed up.

With pressure from his body, I was laid down on his bed. I had an idea of where things were going and even though I didn't want to do anything, I felt like it would be okay. I thought that since I liked him and he knew it, he liked me too. That made me believe that what we were about to do was alright. As I was removing my shorts, he slid his hand up my thighs to part them. Immediately, his fingers entered me. I turned my head and found my eyes connecting to the woman and man on the television. The sound of their pleasure was different than what I remembered from my experience a few years before. She sounded as if she enjoyed the movement of the man that was on top of her as did my best friend who was still having her "moment" with the other guy.

He told me to, "Relax," as he adjusted his body and exchanged his fingers for his penis. The pain was intense yet again. Unlike the prior time, I didn't revert to thoughts of my safe space, I didn't feel the need to run mentally because I was with a guy that I liked and that I assumed had the same feelings for me as I had for him. That time, I thought that I would enjoy what was going on. Mimicking the woman on television, I made the same sounds she did even though I didn't feel the way she was feeling. I kept my eyes on the couple that was in love, or so I thought they were. The noises she made, I too made. The words she said, I repeated. Even though I had no idea what a climax was, I said I was having one after hearing her say the same thing. He genuinely enjoyed himself while I only pretended to do the same.

As I faked my enjoyment, the door to a long sexual addiction had opened. Not only did I become addicted to sex that night but I became addicted to pornography as well. It would be an addiction that would become a thorn in my side for over twenty-five years.

Three times I pleaded with the Lord about this, that it should leave me.
2 Corinthians 12:8 ESV

Yesterday's Trash

The night ended with me leaving his bedroom and going back to his sister's room. My friend remained in the room with him and his best friend. I got in bed next to my friend and went to sleep. The next day, thinking I had just formed a relationship with an older guy, I was shocked to find that he treated me like he'd never known me. When I said hi to him, he would give me a head nod. And once again, I thought I had done something wrong to make him not want to talk to me. I tried to get him to speak to me, but he wouldn't say anything beyond the occasional "Hey," or "I'm good," when I asked him how he was doing.

Not telling my mother what happened was the best way to make sure I didn't get into trouble for kind of choosing to have sex that time. While I thought she would never find out, I was wrong again. She did. My best friend's mother overheard us talking about that night. She told my mother because she didn't want me to end up like her pre-teen daughter. My mom called the police immediately after asking me what happened. I remember him and his mom standing on their back porch which faced our kitchen window. I remember him calling me a lair and saying I was trying to get him in trouble. He yelled at me and called me names.

"What I look like f***ing a fat girl?"
Those words struck me and stuck to me hard.
What would he look like doing so to me?
A fool, I guess. Or it would be beneath him. But he did do the do with a fat girl. That fat girl was me.

My mother had taken me to the doctor to make sure I wasn't pregnant or infected with anything. I remember a lady and a man being in the room with me after one of them told my mom to exit. I don't remember all that was asked, but they did ask me if anyone in my home had forced me to do anything that I didn't want to do. After I answered their questions, my mom was allowed back in the room while they performed the tests. It would be the first time I had a pap smear, at twelve-years-old, which was just as uncomfortable as sex. After swabbing inside of me, they told us the results would be sent to my primary doctor and to follow up with them.

I went home and was placed on a punishment for the rest of the year. I remember it being the month of September when everything happened because as October rolled in, I was told that I wasn't going trick or treating because I was still in trouble. It may not make sense now, but September would forever be a challenging month for me, I'll tell you more about that later.

A few weeks would pass before there was a court date to address what happened between him and me. I remember sitting in the hallway with my mom while he and his mom sat way off from us. I didn't want him to get in trouble, I remember thinking that I would tell the court he didn't do anything that night and that we were just playing. Then maybe he wouldn't be so upset and he would finally talk to me. That wasn't really what I wanted at all though. Honestly, I just wanted him to like me. I wanted him to love me like I needed to be loved. I wanted to be his girlfriend and him to be my boyfriend. I wanted him to want to talk to me and to have a baby with me. I wanted him to see me. But instead, he looked at me and snarled, sending me such a look of disgust.

Lowering my head, I wiped a few tears that tried to run down my face. I stopped them before they could cause my pain to be revealed. When his name and mine were called, my mom waited for him and his mother to walk past us and then said to me, "Wait here."

Doing what she said, I watched her walk into the courtroom followed by the county officer. I don't recall how long they were in the room but when they walked out, he was mumbling something as he and his mom headed to the hallway where the elevators were. My mom approached me, instructing me to follow her as we left. We walked into the same hallway he was in and when he saw me, he looked at me with such disgust and said, "Don't look at me, fat a**." Before my mom could say anything, his mother said something to him in Spanish and shoved him. He replied in the same language while pointing at me.

I could have died.

I believe I did.

I was a walking corpse.

The bell to the elevator dinged and they disappeared when the doors closed behind them. My mom said we would wait for the next elevator to keep us from getting on with them.

When we got back home that afternoon, my mom, talking to one of my aunts, told her what the judge had said to him concerning me. He was told that he had to stay away from me and that if he returned to the courtroom again about having sex with a young girl, he would be put away. It would be odd for him to stay away from me because we lived next door to each other. So, how could we avoid each other? As well, I don't know why he was only given a warning and nothing more. At twelve years old, I couldn't ask for more clarity, I doubt if my mom even knew why things happened the way they did.

As I write this, I am being flooded with the memories of every man that I tried to get to see me, to notice me, to acknowledge me for who I was. I wanted them to see me beyond sex. I needed them to see that I was someone they could spend life with. I wanted them to see that goodness was in my heart, not that it was only between my legs. I wanted to feel loved and the only way I felt that was by giving them what they wanted. It didn't matter if I received what I wanted or not. I did not matter. If they would give me an inch of their attention, I would give them a mile of mine. Oh, how I wish I knew better. How I wish someone had told me that I didn't have to have sex to prove that I was worthy of love. Had someone told me that, my body count would've been far less, if not zero. The only man I would have willingly given myself to would have been my husband.

This Is My New Normal

I don't know about anyone else, but my pornography addiction became my new norm. I think I was around thirteen years old when we got a computer and the internet. Oh boy, was I in perverted heaven. I don't recall how I found it, but when I did, I chased it. I figured out how to search for what I wanted to view. I found site after site after site. I learned how to give myself pleasure that, when it first happened, I didn't know what it was but it caused me to climax. My body craved it. My mind devoured it. My thoughts were stuck on it.

For some reason, I told another friend about what I had found online. Sharing it with her was like sharing candy from a stranger. If I did it, then surely she could too. We would be in the basement, where the computer was, watching countless videos without sound. But I knew what it sounded like because I'd heard it before. I don't know if what I showed her sparked something in her that would stay with her for years, but it felt like I was doing something good to share my newly found feel-good outlet with my friend.

Nothing about what I watched was disturbing to me. It didn't cause me to be afraid of sex or men. My life had become surrounded with the sights and sounds of pornography. Everything I looked at reminded me of sex. If someone yawned, it reminded me of moaning from pleasure. I was sensitive to creating "scenes" in my head that could lead to some random acts of sex. By sensitive I mean, if I was in the bathroom at school, I would think of a guy joining me and us having a quick moment of passion before I went back to class.

Everything I did lead to me viewing my guilt-less pleasure. If I was bored, porn. If I was sleepy, porn. If I felt rejected, porn. If I felt excited about an upcoming event, porn. If I was home alone, porn. If I wasn't alone, porn. And the older I became, the more aggressive my viewing had become. I had it on my laptop, tablet, and cell phone. I had VCR tapes, which for the life of me I don't know how I got them. I swear, it was as if the tapes just appeared. Trust me, they were just there. Just in my reach. I would hurry home from school, from work, or from being with friends just to have a few intimate moments.

When I moved out of my mother's house and into my own, it was over! I would spend a whole day in bed just watching and pleasing myself. I wasn't afraid to get caught by anyone because I was in the privacy of my own home and could do what I wanted. Even when my friend and I got a townhouse together, I would remain in my room and watch with earbuds on to keep anyone from hearing. I would watch and "do me".
I was messed up and didn't know it.
I had no idea just how consumed my life had become.

Longing Effects

They Showed Me No Love, But I Loved Them Anyway.

The heart is the strongest muscle in the body but it's the easiest to be broken. It is what keeps the blood flowing through our body to give us life. Without the heart, we die.

I often felt dead inside due to the series of heart attacks I had as a child. Feeling abandoned and being assaulted two-times had changed me. I wasn't aware of all the effects of those emotional attacks until I began to date around the age of sixteen. It was then that I noticed I would do anything for the love and attention of a boy and how the rejection from that boy, the not getting what I so desired, hurt me even more.

As I'm sharing this part of my story, I am reminded, by the Spirit, of a time in middle school when I liked a boy that didn't like me. I would say hi to him every day, I told my friends I liked him and would buy him ice cream on Fridays when my mom gave me money for my own treats. That boy only spoke to me on those days. The rest of the week, I couldn't get a single peep out of him.

It wasn't until I heard him say, "I don't like you," that I began not to retreat from him as one would expect, but to be drawn to him even more. I was certain that he just didn't know me well yet, and that if I showed him that I was a nice girl, he

44

would like me. I couldn't think of any other way to show him what he couldn't see except by using my body.

Yea, my body.

I had developed early and was top-heavy for most of my life. Having big breast as a young girl drew the attention of boys and adult men. I never paid the men any mind, but the boys I gave my attention to. One day I told that boy I would let him see and touch my breasts if he said he liked me.

What preteen or teenage boy would have turned that offer down?

I remember we were in the stairwell between classes, how we got away with being alone like that I do not know, but we did. Staying true to my word, I lifted my shirt and let him see me. I was sure, downright confident, that I would finally have the boy I liked because I would give him something he wanted even though he hadn't asked for it. As his hands caressed my breasts, I closed my eyes and went to my safe place, my bedroom. I don't know what prompted him to do what he did next, but suddenly and unexpectedly he began to put his mouth on my breasts. When he did, I jumped because it startled me. I was not expecting that, I only wanted him to touch me.

Covering myself up, I asked him, "Do you like me now?"

He stared at me and said a very vehement, "No!" then ran up the stairs and disappeared around a corner. I was lost and confused. I thought boys like that kind of stuff. So, if I did what boys liked, then surely they would like me.

I was wrong.

See, no one ever told me that neither love nor like was found between my legs. No one never shared with me how special I was and how I didn't have to prove to the boys that they should like me for any reason beyond who I was. I wish I knew then what I know now. I would have saved myself years of uncomfortable sexual encounters, time spent trying to get a guy to call me his own.

I guess being in search of what I was lacking caused me to not care how it came to me, just that it did.

Chatline of "Love"

When I was around the age of sixteen, I met a guy on the local chatline. He was so kind to me over that phone and made me feel special with his words. When I found out where he lived, which was around the corner and two-blocks over, we agreed to meet up. I told my mother that I was going to spend the night at my friend's house for the weekend, but I lied. Well, not completely. I spent that Friday night with him, then Saturday with my friend. She covered for me and since her mother worked overnights, it wasn't a hardship to get away with that lie.

When I arrived at his house, I was nervous but kept a smile on my face, thinking that I had found a guy to really like me for me. He told me how beautiful I was and how happy I made him. He told me, at sixteen, that he could marry me and take care of me. I believed him. Everything in me believed he cared the way he said he did, especially since his actions, thus far, supported his words. The night we spent together was so sweet. We had dinner, watched tv, and then I showered before going to bed. When I finally lay down with him, he was gentle with me. I didn't feel forced or like a piece of meat. I felt loved. I felt wanted. I felt needed. I felt everything I wanted to feel with a man.
Oh, did I mention that he was in his early twenties?

He had an apartment that he shared with his sister. I don't recall why she wasn't there that night, but it didn't matter because he and I had our private time together. I could go into details about the night but there wouldn't be a point because when morning came and I left, it seemed as though, within the span of a few hours, everything had changed.

Before I left him to head to my friend's house, he told me to page him later that afternoon. I did. We spoke briefly before he had to go, and that would be the last time I heard from him. I did what people today call, 'blow up his phone,' but it was his pager back then. See, I didn't have a direct number to him, I only had his pager number. Let me explain how that happened just in case you're wondering. When we met on the chatline, he asked

me for my number and when he called me, he had blocked his number. Each time he called it was from a blocked number. So, the only way I could reach him was with his pager number.
Sad, I know.

That entire weekend had gone from wonderful to a dread for me. I couldn't understand what I had done wrong, what I had done to make a man that said he wanted to marry me kick me to the curb after spending a beautiful night with me. It didn't make sense to me how he wanted me in his life one minute and the next minute he didn't even want to keep me around. The more I tried to figure out what I could have possibly done wrong, the lower I felt. It would take a few months for me to get over him. The sound of his voice, the kindness of his touch, they both lingered. I wanted to feel that way again, you know, loved, cared for, supported, needed, wanted. I wanted that for a lifetime.
Although that night with him would not be the last of that kind with other men, there were only few men that changed my life with the way they loved me. Even though their way was not how I wanted to be loved, I was just glad someone wanted to.

Year-to-Date

Nothing could have prepared me for the years I spent trying to get boys and men to just see me. I was invisible to the naked eyes of men that only wanted to see me naked. When I say "see me", I mean see me for the person I was and am. I mean, see me as someone that is more than just the object of sexual desire and fulfillment. See me.

Older now, I see that I was only begging for them to want me even when I didn't want myself. I wanted them to appreciate what I didn't have value in... Me!

The Doors Too Hard to Close
Door #1: September's Residue

The residue of abuse in any fashion is something that doesn't easily wash away. It remains for a lifetime, clinging to your soul and somehow finding its way into every decision you make. It shapes your attitude, your outlook and, in some, creates a sense of needing to control everything. The residue leaves its smudges in our relationships, our love expressions, and how we communicate with others.

For me, there were many areas of my life effected by the residue of sexual abuse, but I didn't come to that conclusion until early 2020. It was in the moments of being in a dark place that it become clear what the root of it all was. It wasn't an easy revelation to come to, but it was worth it. As I mentioned earlier, I was sexually abused at twelve years old. Well, because that door had been opened, it allowed some lifelong baggage to come in, baggage I would carry for over twenty-five years, and every September I would unpack it.

Can I break right here and tell you that as I type this my heart is pounding in my ears? I am afraid to share this, but the inner most part of me is whispering, sweetly in my ear, drowning out my beating heart, "I Am with you. All is well."

For so long whenever September rolled around, I would begin to feel out of place. I would feel like something inside of me was off balance, didn't belong, and it caused me to become uncertain about many things. Like, I knew who I was, but this thing made me doubt myself. When I was employed, I would feel like I wasn't good enough to be there and would begin comparing myself to my co-workers. I would become stuck in my head about my lack of experience, which was crazy because I have over twenty-years of customer service experience and was with that company for twelve of those twenty-five years. But every September, my work performance would begin to suffer greatly. It was around that time of year that I would show up to work late, answer the phones with a bad or sad attitude. Some people would get the brunt of my anger and annoyance, emotions that would come out of nowhere. I remember not wanting to talk to anyone until ten a.m. whereas work started at eight a.m. I would begin to hate my life and feel as though I wanted to leave this place. Thank God I had the thoughts of my mom and sister to keep me from ending it all. I didn't want them to find my body or be forced to identify it, so I didn't do it for their sake. The suicidal thoughts actually ended when I became saved. I guess He awarded me with a reason to live despite longing for death in the prior years.

As time would go on, I would become increasingly saddened by what was or wasn't going on around me. Once October rolled in, I would feel down, uninspired, lacking interest in my normal everyday life. I would sleep often and wake up as if I never did. I was foggy in my mind, meaning I couldn't think clearly. I was withdrawn from family and friends, not wanting to do anything. When I had to go out, it was a push and pull for me to do so. I would try to come up with every excuse in the 1001 Excuses Not to Go Out hand guide, any excuse that would allow me to stay home.

Sometimes, I wouldn't go without giving an excuse, other times I would make one up. Then there were times I would go to an event and be like a fly on the wall. I wouldn't interact with anyone or say much until finally I just found my way out the door, to my car, and then home. Trick or Treating didn't excite me either. All joy would fade and sorrow would become my way of life.

After October was finished with me, November and December would take over and not let go! Those were the worst months of the year for me. Those months reminded me of everything I felt my life lacked.

November 14: I turned a year older. Still single. Still childless.

Thanksgiving: Still single. Still unmarried. Still watching my family and friends grow while I remained stagnate.

Christmas Season: Still single. Still unmarried. Still childless.

New Year: Another year has come and gone, 365 days of being single, unmarried and childless.

See, all those years past, I thought my sadness was due to what I didn't have but desired, to be married with children. Yet, that wasn't it. Even if God had given me what my heart desired, I still wouldn't have been happy or satisfied because the root of the truth hadn't be dealt with yet.

Have you ever heard of muscle memory? Similar to that, my 'body memory' remembered that September night which caused the four to five months downward spiral. I unconsciously allowed the memory and the things that followed shift my life every year thereafter. It may not seem like much to you, but to me, those were hard months to live through, and the thought of them coming back around sent me into panic mode. I called it seasonal depression because it only lasted for a season out of the year.

I could feel the changes coming in August, then in September those changes would be a full blown "seasonal depression." You might be thinking, "Well, Ebony, a lot of people have seasonal depression." Yes, that's correct, but the depression isn't the only door that was opened when my body was stolen from me. Many things entered into my life that would have rule over me longer than I had been alive.

Depression is, sadly, common for many people. Some live with it, some die from it. I chose to live even if doing so was the bare minimum of my existence. I had to fight to able to function, to smile, to give my life a chance to thrive and to love me for the very first time. It wasn't until I began to really devote the broken pieces of me to God and allow, ask, and respectfully demand, Him to have His way in my life. The funny part is that the broken pieces were all of me. Every area of my life had brokenness in it. Some pieces were larger, more jagged than others while very few pieces were smooth due to smooth breaks. The easiest thing for me to do was hide what was really going on with me. I couldn't tell anyone because I was afraid of what they would think of me, feel towards me, and even worse, I was afraid they wouldn't understand me.

I was alone in my despair. Broken. Hidden. Shunned in my thoughts. It all was a part of the baggage that I unpacked every September. It would spill out and lie around my life until the end of the year. That was the routine journey that life had taken me on. Yet, as 2020 rolled in, the baggage wasn't put away. It had a hidden zipper that only God was aware of, and that zipper had broken, and the contents shattered my once private life came tumbling out.

Another Door Too Heavy for Me to Close
Door #2: The 25-Year Opened Door

Well, it was my addiction...
I was addicted to...
For over twenty-years I was addicted to pornography.
Father, for Your glory, do I expose myself.

Have you picked your mouth up off the floor yet? I know. I know.
Let me give you the space to allow your head to wrap around what you just read.

Women being addicted to pornography is new to many, but for me it was the norm. Let me take you back to the twelve-year-old Ebony that had to bear the weight of rape and molestation alone, without a voice to acknowledge or deal with any of it. Maybe that will explain why and how it was normal for me and how God delivered me from it. I hope you're ready because I'm crying and screaming out to God as I type these words. I'm happy to be free to open my mouth about what held me hostage for most of my life.

The second time I was touched began with us watching pornography. At that time, I wasn't aware of what it was. I had no idea that watching a VHS, which I would forget to rewind causing an uproar in our house, was the gateway to something more damaging. I didn't know that what I didn't know how to do could be taught to me in a sixty-minute video. I didn't know that I could stop, rewind, slow down a particular part to make sure I got it right. I didn't know that I would long for the pleasure of watching and the gratification that accompanied it.

The rape occurred because I wasn't ready to do what the woman was doing to the man. Since he was aroused and I had no way of getting out of what I was in, he did what he wanted to get what he needed.

I don't recall where I obtained that tape, but I had gotten my hands on my own personal VHS tape of pornography. Since my mom had purchased a VSH player that was my very own, I could watch it at my leisure to satisfy my yearning flesh. I remember showing it to my friends who, like me, marveled at what we were watching. I, not sure if they were or not, was amazed at what I saw. I didn't have to use my imagination to think about sex because I was watching it "live" in front of me, on my television with the volume on mute.

My nights were spent alone in the attic that had been converted into my bedroom. Away from prying ears, I learned to muffle the sounds that creeped up my throat and to my lips. Silence wasn't too hard to learn because at eight I'd been hushed and told not to make any noise. As a result, remaining silent while rubbing my own hands across my private nerves wasn't difficult. I was a young girl, watching, participating in, becoming addicted to pornography.

As technology advanced, so did access to my chosen viewing pleasure. For the life of me, it alludes me how I became aware of the ability to watch what was once only on my tv, now on my desktop. I do, however, remember using the internet to search for my favorite genre, if I may, of sex. Before this knowledge was dropped on me, I used to surf for ways to download pirated music from my favorite artist. Now, I searched for ways to pirate what aroused me, what caused a river to flow and tingles in my toes.

This went on year after year. The wider the internet became, the wider my search for what I wanted to see. I would spend hours upon hours searching, watching, pleasing myself only to be back at it again. I couldn't tell you how many viruses my desktop kept getting. I think I was "cleaning" it a few times a week. I would be eighteen years old when I determined that in order for me to "find pleasure" with my boyfriend, a porno had to be playing. We had to watch it for my benefit. He had to keep up with a man he didn't even know he was competing with. He couldn't stop before the man on the screen. If he did, I would become upset and angry. And I really man angry. It wasn't a healthy relationship by any stretch of the imagination. He wanted me to perform and I wanted him to. The both of us failed each other on many occasions.

To make this shorter and lessen the time to take you through the last twenty plus years, I'll sum it up as this: sex to me was a temporary pleasure designed to erase the pain of the touch that stole my innocence. I used sex to cover the hurt that sex caused. It doesn't make much sense to others, but it does to me. I believe I tried to take back what was stolen by enjoying it freely. Pornography was the tool that helped me to enjoy what I hadn't liked when it originally happened. Watching those scenes taught me that it was okay to have a man's hands on my body, his lips in places my doctor hadn't seen yet. It was my way of seeing that my body was mine and that I could choose what I wanted to do with it. I was wrong for so long. I would never find peace in finding the pieces of me scattered across so many men, meaning I wanted to be healed from it all but I only found myself in the arms of strange men and meaningless relationships.

The shocker that may cause some issues is that I become a saved woman on December 31, 2011. In November of 2017 is when healing from the rape and the molestation finally began. Yes, I was saved and addicted to pornography. I raised my hands in glory and lowered my hand to pleasure myself. It was at the end of 2017 that God really began a good work in me, but it didn't come to completion until 2020. See, there are levels to God's work. He shared this with me as He compared it to the children of Israel being loosed from Pharaoh.

Healing – this takes place when you are really ready to move past what has kept you bound for so long. Hurt and pain of yester-year has done its work and now you want what you deserve: freedom. (Exodus 13)

Deliverance – after you are healed from what caused you so much distress, you have to be removed from it so it doesn't impact your life anymore. The pain points no longer affect you. (Exodus 14)

Set Free – bondage is no longer a thing for you. No more wearing it as a coat of armor. You have taken back the power that once held you hostage and caused you to lose your voice to speak. It also gives you a small voice that grows as you reclaim yourself. (Joshua 1)

I was healed from the sexual abuse. I was free to write and talk about it, but I wasn't delivered. Although my pain points weren't tender any longer, fruit that the root produced continued. I was filled with promise and perversion at the same time. I knew that what I was doing was wrong and went against everything God said, but my flesh, my flesh would not let me go. I resorted to watching it only when many weeks would pass and I needed a release. There were many nights I would feel horrible about it, but sooner than later I'd find myself in that same position.

There is more I could share about it, but I think this is enough.

As I'm writing this, God said to me, after I struggled for so long to be let go from this demon, "This is the last piece that has you bound." Not telling my story had me constrained by a private shame and a spiritual affliction. So, I

> God wants us to be amazed, not surprised when He does just what He promised He would do.
> – Andre Crouch

am releasing this with the faith that it is for His glory as I try to keep my head up high. I don't know what will come of this, but I do know that I am finally free. Free from fighting the battle that has been raging for decades and finally free to close the door to the thing that followed me from year to year.

I believe the moment I sent this chapter off was the very moment I was delivered and set free from pornography.

Section Two: Warning Signs

As with men, women's most common heart attack symptom is chest pain or discomfort. Women don't always get the same classic heart attack symptoms as men, such as crushing chest pain that radiates down one arm. They are somewhat more likely than men to experience some of the other common symptoms, particularly shortness of breath, nausea/vomiting and back or jaw pain. Many experiences vague or even "silent" symptoms that they may miss.

Hopeful

I remember the first day we met. I was walking from the bus stop after working my four-hour shift at KFC. I was seventeen years old and couldn't work too many hours, but those measly hours were enough for my empty pockets. The afternoon was warm and breezy, I enjoyed the kisses from the wind because my uniform was extremely hot. The thickness of the shirt made me sweat even more. Nearly home, I thought about how I would shower, change out of those hot clothes, and hang out for the rest of that summer day. I was also wondering what it would cost me to get a car and if working my cashier's job would be enough for me to get one and pay the car insurance.

As I played with the idea of having my own four wheels to get me to work, school, and to house parties with my friends, my thoughts were interrupted by squeaky wheels coming from a bike followed by, "Hey."

I looked to my left to find a skinny, brown skin boy riding a ten-speed bike in the street as I walked on the sidewalk. Not wanting to be rude, and because he was cute, I smiled at him. "Hey," I replied and turned to complete my long trek home. At that point I noticed he didn't keep riding past me but was now going in my direction at my pace.

"You're cute and I like your gap," he said. Then I remember he almost fell off his bike when he, for some reason, began to swerve. I assumed he was trying to be cool or something, I do not know. But what I do know is that I was surprised by his comment. I had never been told that someone liked my gap. I usually got stares or the random, "You're missing a tooth?"

Ugh!

Anyways.

Because my gap was an inherited trait from my late father's side of the family, specifically my granny, I only felt comfortable smiling around that side of my family. It was as if I really belonged and wouldn't be teased about my gap or asked annoying questions about it. My granny told me when I was a kid, "Don't cover your smile. Do you see me covering mine?" I shook my head no, to which she replied, "Than don't you cover yours." However, I didn't listen to my granny about my smile. I kept my head low enough to try and hide my gap. I would talk in a manner so that my lips would hide my gap and when I laughed, I would cover my smile. I was a determined young woman, determined to keep my smile hidden. Apparently, I hadn't hid it enough from him.

At first, I thought he was being funny or just teasing me like I'd been teased in the past, but he was serious. He said, "My mom has gap and I love her smile."

I don't know why I was shocked, but I was. I wondered, but didn't ask, if she was of the same family blood line as me seeing it was such a prominent trait in my family.

"Oh," was all I could say to him because I really had no other words.

Beside the fact he liked my gap, he also said I was cute.

Cute.

Cute.

Me.

Ebony Nicole.

Cute.

The one that had been rejected by the boys she liked through middle and high school. That Ebony was cute. Not the one that had been called fat when she told a boy she liked him. Not that

Ebony was cute. I know it sounds crazy, but I believe it was in those moments that I began to fall for men's words instead of their actions. For someone who was used to never being told she was cute, except from family, which I didn't think counted, it was foreign to my ears and pleasing.

"Thank you. You're cute too." And he was.

He was this skinny kid with long legs and a beautiful smile. His brown skin was shimmering under the summer sun and his out of shape t-shirt hung on his body showing a hint of muscles, or it could have just been bones because he really was a skinny kid.

As I continued to walk while he rode his bike, he asked for my name, where I was going and coming from. He told me his name and said he was just riding around. He then asked if he could walk with me to my house, which I told him was okay. For a few moments, we were silent. I don't know what he was thinking but I was thinking that a boy thought I was cute and I didn't even like him first. Go figure.

When we reached my home, he mentioned that he lived up the street from me. And by the up the street, he meant just that. Up the street. From my house it was about a five-minute walk to his house. Then he told me he wanted to see me later, which I agreed to. We stood outside for a hot few minutes before I went inside to get out of my clothes. Before I did that, I watched him ride away and as he did, "Bye, cutie," was said to me.

To me.

I was a cutie for the first time ever.

Me. A cutie.

Let me pause for a moment to share this: tell your daughters, nieces, sisters, cousins, kids of friends, anyone and everyone, little girl, young woman, and woman that she is beautiful and tell her what you think is such about her. Not hearing it will cause her to fall for a boy or man that tells her, for the first time, something she's never heard. Becoming used to being told that you're beautiful will, I hope, keep her from feeling like a guy is extra special and deserves something just as much because of his words.

To be honest, as I write the book and have to recall the relationship with him, I don't know if it was him that I fell for or if it was his words. He did nothing to deserve to have me as his girlfriend. He didn't have to work hard, buy a gift, take me anywhere, be supportive or anything to make me feel like he would be a good guy to me. I guess when you're not aware of how to date, how to know when it's love you feel, anything works. He was just what I needed to boost my self-esteem and to make me finally feel seen.

Whatever it was that made me like him, granted him access to my secret space. He was the first guy that I allowed to have me. There was no need to fight, be afraid, or cry. I wasn't uncomfortable either. I remember one night we were hanging out at his house. It was me and his two little sisters. His mother was a drug addict, so she was very rarely home at night. He had put in a video for his sisters to watch and told them that we were going in his room to watch a different movie. We didn't watch a move let alone turn on the tv.

I don't know how long it lasted but I enjoyed my boyfriend, I enjoyed having someone that liked me, that wanted to be with me and wanted to do what he referred to as, "Make love." Honestly, it was the first time I had "made love," which is odd because I was not in love with him at that time. I was in love with the idea that someone wanted me in a good way. I was in love with the idea of a boyfriend that chose me first. He would become my first of many things, but not the last.

The First to Get a Prayer

I used to think we could spend forever together. Being that it was my senior year of high school, I was excited to have a boyfriend that last year. Finally reaching my peak in high school, I assumed things would only get better from there. Since I had decided to attend college, the thought of having a boyfriend that could come visit me was exciting. But before we could get to the end of the school year, we celebrated then departed from each other.

His birthday arrived in late October, and to show him how much I loved him—again, not sure if I really did—I had a little surprise for him, one he'd never experienced before. Since it was Halloween, I picked up a cake that had orange frosting and a black and white ghost on it. Across the top of it was his name and Happy Birthday. I also grabbed a gallon of ice cream and some chips. I remember my mom and little sister came to his house with me, it was the first time my mom and his mom met.

When he saw the cake, he fought back tears. Hugging me, he whispered, "This is the first time I ever had a cake." He'd turned nineteen years old that day. It surprised me greatly that he'd never had a cake to celebrate him the prior eighteen years. Because of him, I made sure to celebrate the birth of every man I dated after that. I wanted him to feel special because he was such to me. I wanted him to know that I was happy for his life and that he had made it with me being in it. I wanted him to feel as if someone cared beyond just him caring for himself. I can only remember the many smiles I left behind now.

My birthday was the following month, November. The biggest moment I remember was that since I had turned eighteen, I was able to work longer hours at my job. I was happy about it because it meant I could start saving for everything that I wanted to get for my senior year. My mom had already told me that I had to cover it all because we didn't have the money, so I was excited to make more money.

Celebrating myself had become a thing I'd done ever since I was fourteen. It didn't bother me if I'd gotten a gift because I was a gift to myself. I had a house party and invited a bunch of friends over. I remember we were up in my room in the attic, and at the end of the night it was only he and I left. We had sex and he went to sleep.

I remember slipping out of bed, going to the foot of it, and falling on my knees. The tv was on and the light emanating from it was the only light that shined on his resting body. I don't know all that I prayed but I remember asking God to watch over him. The funny thing is, I didn't know God to even ask Him to do me a favor like watch over my boyfriend. I like to believe that something in all of us know God is real, but we can choose to know and acknowledge Him or not. Getting back in bed, I kissed his lips which aroused him awake. I snuggled up to him and went back to bed, but not before having sex, again.

All the major holidays that meant the world to me arrived with my man by my side. Life could not be better because for once, I felt seen by a guy that really wanted me. It felt good and there wasn't anything I wouldn't do to keep him and that feeling.

Well, almost anything.

Let the Truth Be Revealed

I do not know how much I worked to pay for prom, senior trip, senior pictures, college applications, cap and gown, hair, and makeup, but I did. As I was searching for and applying to colleges, he had decided to attend the Community College. I was proud of him, excited that he would be reaching for greater and higher heights just as I was. He asked me to help him figure it all out since I was doing the same for myself. It was a great start to the rest of our lives. We just had to get through my last year of school, then we could move on to more.

The year seemed to breeze by because before I knew it, the details about prom had been announced. I had already assumed my man would be the one taking me.

Wrong!

About a month before prom, he told me he would get a tux and a limo for us to arrive in style in. I believed him although, thinking about it now, he didn't have a job! Nevertheless, I planned for prom. I offered to help him pay for what he needed to do, but he declined. Weeks away from the big night, my mom and I went to JC Penny to pick out a dress and shoes. I found someone to do my hair and makeup. The only thing I was waiting on was confirmation from him that he was all set. I would ask him often, and he would tell me that he was working on it.

I tried not to nag him, but he couldn't tell me where he was getting the tux from or the limo. Despite my better judgement, I believed in him. I believed that he was working on it because he knew how important that day was going to be for me. I believed that the man that loved me was going out to his way just for me. Maybe it was the feeling of being hopeful that kept me holding on with the lack of proof. I had to learn the hard way about all proof not being required for me to see it. I just needed to hear it to change my mind about a thing.

One day my mom came home yelling my name. I was in my room asleep and jumped up when she called out for me. I remember her saying, "He cheatin' on you. I saw him with a girl pushing a stroller." At first, I didn't feel anything because I knew he had a son, but it was what was said about me that bothered me the most.

My mother told me she pulled over and asked him what he was doing, to which he replied, "Nothing." I don't know what happened in between, but my mom told the baby's mother that he was at our house the night before. The girl began to argue with him before he blurted out, as he pointed to my mom, "She's my ex-girlfriend's mother. We're not together!"

Those words shook me to my core. I was hurt and began to cry. Turning back to go to my room, I heard my mom's boyfriend say, "Those dudes up the street ain't no good."

It was the first time that a guy I loved broke my heart. I couldn't believe I was being played by someone that chose me first. Days passed before he showed up at my house with his favorite cousin, trying to explain why he said I was his ex. His cousin had a lot to add to the conversation and to the excuses too.

I remember him saying, "Your mom didn't know what was going on. They could have been taking the baby to a doctors' appointment."

Hmmm. Could have, but I doubted it.

The explanation my boyfriend offered up was that she was crazy and jealous and if she knew he had a girlfriend she wouldn't allow him to see his son. I was a young girl, I didn't know girls would use a kid like a pawn. So, I didn't believe him anymore. He could have told me the world stopped spinning and I would trust his word. He could have told me that the sun was falling slowly and I would have believed every word. Yet, when it came to cheating, I couldn't do it. My mind shifted quickly the moment I heard my mom tell me the story of what she saw. Having him with his son's mother bothered me because I, too, wanted to have his baby. The desire to be a mother had grown in me when I was younger. It was something I wanted for no other reason than to have someone love me without conditions or reservations.

I was hopeful that we would one day have a family, but that one day would never come. I broke up with him right before prom. I decided that I would go alone until my best friend's older brother said he wanted to go and would buy his own ticket. I was cool with that because he was like a big brother to me.

I felt like everything had fallen apart in such a short time. I went from planning for my future to wondering if I would ever have one with a guy that wanted to be true to me. Puppy love is what it's called when you're young and in love. And many would say not to count it as real love for that reason. I counted as real love because parts of me had come to life from being with him. The desire to care for a man, to support him in his endeavors and to listen and believe more in his words than his actions sprung forth. I would carry those desires for years to come. If I could help him accomplish something then I felt needed, wanted, and valid in his life. It would be these desires that would cause me to be attracted to men who were in need beyond my capacity to help.

Hope Fulfilled

Off the heels of my first heartbreak, I finished high school and headed to college. Ready to start my life and become as great as I could be, I was happy to be away from home. I did miss my mom and my sister but being out of Rochester and meeting new people made it comfortable.

One thing I was happy about is that my manager at KFC allowed me to work when I returned home on breaks. During the Thanksgiving break in 2001, I remember working the nightshift the day after the holiday. It was a slow night because people where still out shopping and enjoying holiday leftovers. Towards the end of my shift, I was cleaning up the back area where food was prepped when I heard my manager call out my name. Heading to the front, I saw a tall, black guy standing at my register. We had a bulletproof window inside the store because it was constantly being robbed. Thank God it never happened while I was there.

Welcoming him to the restaurant, I proceeded to take his order, prepare it, and hand it over to him. He thanked me and sat down in the back corner. At first, I didn't pay him any attention, I had already decided not to bother with a boyfriend because it did my heart no justice. I don't recall if I even noticed how attractive he was. I was focused on cleaning up the restaurant, waiting for my mom to come get me from work, getting home and going to bed. It had been a long day.

After I was finished with the back area, I grabbed the mop and bucket and filled it up. Then I grabbed the broom and a cloth and headed to the front dining room. I wiped down the tables, except the one he was at, and then swept the floor. I was going to mop after he left and the doors were locked. My plan was flawless because I was used to doing it. My manager instructed me to lock one of the two entry doors since we had about twenty-minutes left in the shift. As I did, the guy approached the counter again. I went back to the register to take another order from him. I packed him another meal and handed it to him. I told him to have a great night.

Before walking away he asked, "What's your name?" I told him and he said that he was wondering if he could have my number. To be honest, when he asked my name, I thought he wanted it so he could leave a review for my exceptional customer service. That was what I was used to from customers. Being asked my name and then following that up with asking for my number was not the norm. I remember staring at him and smiling before using the receipt paper to write my number on.

Taking that paper, he left and said he would call me the next day. When he left, my manager, in her thick Jamaican accent said, "Oh, Elbany. That's your new boyfriend."

I walked past her, laughing as I headed to the dining area to clean up behind him. Surprisingly, he had either cleaned up his own mess or he hadn't made one. I locked the second door, mopped the floor, and stood by my manager as she counted and closed my drawer for the evening. She then ran her daily report, while I deboned a bucket of chicken from earlier in the day to be used for the chicken pot pies the next day. Just after ten pm, my mom arrived, and I left.

I didn't expect to hear from him at all. I was busy enjoying my business and making some money before leaving a couple of days later. For a long while, even as an adult, I would just give my number to a guy without expectation. I found that having no expectation of men when it came to me was best. From relationship to relationship, my thoughts were supported by their behavior. It would be years before that would be debunked.

The next night, I was watching television with my mom when the phone rang. Answering it, my mom asked who it was and then handed the cordless phone to me.

"Hello?" Once again, I wasn't expecting a call from anyone.

"Hi, Ebony. This William." He sounded different over the phone. His voice was a lot deeper than it sounded in person, or maybe it was just me not remembering his voice from the night before. Then and there I decided to take the phone to my room for privacy and I'm glad I did.

We talked about everything under the sun and over the moon. He told me about his family life, and I did the same. I told him about school and why I was there. He talked about his job at the car wash and the tips he would make from working. What he hated the most about the job was drying large trucks and the driver giving him a dollar for doing so. He hoped that a minimum tip would have been suggested but it wasn't possible then.

Our first call lasted until the cordless phone began to beep as it ran out of juice. I didn't want to end it and neither did he. I quickly told him I was leaving to head back to school the next day and wanted to see him. He said the same and offered to meet me at the Greyhound Bus Station one-hour before I was to leave. Hanging up the phone, all I could do was smile and giggle. I felt hopeful with him after just after a few hours. I didn't allow my thoughts to pull me ahead of time into the future, but I did think about seeing him and what I would do when I did. Would we hug or just shake hands? Should I kiss him on the lips or on the cheek? I was a silly eighteen-year-old girl filled with the possibilities of life. I was excited to see what these possibilities would bring.

I was eager to get to the bus station to see him again. He called me that morning I was to leave, telling me he had to work but would be there so see me off. For him, my expectation was kind of high. I think it was because he called me to confirm he was coming and didn't give me a reason why he could not. I felt like he wasn't going to let me down so when I arrived at the bus station, I hopped out the car, grabbed my things, kissed and hugged my mom goodbye, and waited for him to arrive. I didn't have a cellphone, so it wasn't possible for me to text him to see where he was or for him to tell me he was on the way. All I had was hope that he would follow through with his words.

As the hour ticked down, the ticket taker announced that the bus was twenty minutes out and that if we needed a ticket, to see her at the counter. Suddenly, I felt let down. The bus was coming, and he wasn't anywhere in sight. All the hope I had in him was deflating the expectation bubble I had blown up in my head. With nothing to do but wait for the time to board to come, I walked outside of the terminal and stood against a concrete pillar. I sat my duffle bag to the side of me and pulled my ticket out of my purse. Holding it so I could show it to the driver, I was startled when my duffle bag was picked up from next to me.

Rising from against the pillar, I said, "What the he…" It was William.

I wrapped my arms around him, and he wrapped his free arm around me. I was so happy to see him. All worry went out the door as I was in his embrace. Fear of the past didn't have a chance to take root in my heart. He came right on time. He arrived just before I could think, "All me are the same." My black night in brown skin saved me that late afternoon. And that first time would not be the last.

With only moments left to spare, just as the ticket taker announced over the PA that my bus was arriving, I stepped back from him to take in the full view of the man I had fallen for after one call. I remember his broad shoulders that carried the weight of a man that was still mourning the loss of his mother five years prior. The frame of his body carried the weight of the good cooking his aunt made every Sunday, and his arms and hands would become a safe space for me. His legs would later find themselves entangled with mine as we lay in each other's arms, hot and sweaty.

The screeching of the bus's brakes snapped me out of what I wanted to do to him. Since I was limited in my available actions, I settled for a kiss. Coming closer to him, he knew what I wanted to do because he sat my bag down, opened his arms, and held tightly to my waist as we kissed for the first time. Passion. Excitement. Newness. Hope. Safety was found in his kiss. I heard the people saying their goodbyes to others, but the beating of my heart was louder. I wasn't afraid. I was brave enough to trust again. I had it set in my heart, a change of heart, to open me once more.

We broke our trance when the bus driver said, "Last call to NYC,' which was not where I was going, but the school was en route to NYC. We walked to the driver's door, he handed the man my duffle bag and gave me a card. He told me to read it once I was on the road and I did. I said to him that I would call once I was settled in my dorm room and I did after I called my mom first. A quick kiss and I was on board the bus for a five hour ride.

Once we hit the throughway to our next stop, I opened his card. I still remember it to this day. It was a generic brand card with a light yellow and white flower on the front with the words, "For someone special." Opening it, I smiled at the sight of his handwritten note on the left side of it. I think I remember the outside because it reminded me of a summer day. I don't recall all that was written but I do remember the words, 'Will you be my girlfriend?' Before I knew Christ, I use to swear, not a lot, but those words did find their way up and out of my mouth. It was one of those words I used to express my joy for him wanting to be my man and for me to be his girl. The funny thing about it was, as quick as I fell for him, it appeared he had done the same for me.

It is said that when a man knows, he doesn't waste any time. Being that we were just kids, I was eighteen and he had just turned twenty, I didn't allow myself to think far into the future as I had done before. Something kept me in the present and I'm glad it did because my imagination could build an entire future from nothing but a few words.

Love Flies, Time Flies

The first year of us together flew by quickly. Before I knew it, we were celebrating our anniversary at his house. He had prepared a dinner of steak and mashed potatoes and broccoli. I can remember the steak being so good because I asked him what he'd done it. He said he cooked it in butter and garlic. And to this very day, when I make steak, I use a lot of butter and garlic to do so. We were in the kitchen with candlelight shimmering between us and with a single red rose just for me.

After dinner, we retreated to his room to enjoy the rest of our night together. Trying to be "grown-ish" at nineteen, I had purchased a silk, red "teddy", as they were called, for the night. After slipping into it in the bathroom, I felt amazing because of the way he watched as I entered his room. I was nervous because I hadn't put on something so sexy ever before. See, I was a big girl then and was self-aware of that fact. But he made me feel good about myself. Not just by how he looked at me but by how he spoke to me and how he handled me with care. There wasn't anything I would not do for him to make sure he kept doing what he did to and for me.

The night of our anniversary, he made me a Queen for real. Laying me down on his bed, he took his time with me. Having nowhere to go in the morning, he spent the night exploring my large frame with his lips. He kissed me, literally, from my forehead to my toes. He kissed parts of me that I didn't know were ticklish and in other areas he spent more time teasing me to make my body shake. To be honest, that was what love making was and how it should have felt. The way he carried for me that night was the first and last time. He wasn't selfish, in a rush, or distracted. He cared that I had reached my climax a few times, was slow in his passionate love for me, and kept his focus on me.

Enough.

Love flies and time flies when you're with someone you want, need and desire. It flies even faster when the feelings are mutual.

My Voice Mattered

Of everything I had the chance to experience with him, it was the arguments that made me feel heard. I know it sounds crazy, but he never let me shutdown in the middle of a disagreement.

Since I was a little girl, whenever conversations would become too hard due to elevated emotions, I would stop talking and just agree with whatever the issue was. Feeling totally different, I didn't want to cause further arguments that would lead to an aggressive action towards me. It's not that I didn't want to express how I felt, I was afraid of what could follow if I did.

It was what I saw growing up. If one person started yelling and the other matched the tone and level of hostility, fists would start swinging. From that, I learned to stop talking when I felt myself beginning to match the emotional position of the other person. It wasn't something I did just in relationships, I did it in school too. I wasn't a fighting girl, I didn't know how to fight and was afraid to be hit. I kept my mouth shut so as not to have someone feel the need to throw a fist my way. I was a scaredy cat. The last time I'd gotten into a fight I was in the fifth grade and was beaten up... Soooo, yeah, no!

But with William, he would tell me to explain to him what was wrong with me. And every time I did, he listened. He listened to understand, not to respond. He paid attention to what I was saying so he could fix what was wrong, or at least offer up an explanation to my response. I wasn't dismissed as, "doing too much," or "overreacting for nothing." With him, my voice mattered. My opinion mattered. For a little while, life allowed me to express myself with my words. Life allowed me a glimpse of standing up for myself instead of cowering over in a corner like a little frightened kitty cat.

I was safe with him. William didn't yell at me or talk down to me. He chose his words wisely to not hurt me and to not cut me deep with them. Whenever we got into an argument, we talked it out and that kept us from allowing our attitudes to fester with hate and it kept us from treating each other like enemies instead of lovers.

With other men after him, I wasn't able to share how I felt because they didn't give me a safe place to share my voice. As I mentioned before, I would be dismissed, told I had taken the comment the wrong way, or how I felt was never addressed in a supportive and understanding way. It would be years before I was given my voice back and made to feel that it mattered.

Thinking about it even more now reminds me of how the Holy Spirit speaks to me. He is loving, kind, and patient. He doesn't force me to talk, instead He leads me do so with tenderness and encouragement. The Holy Spirit offered me, too, a place of safety where my words and voice mattered.

Slipped Away in the Morning

The morning was cool as the warm air breezed through the second-floor window of our dorm room. It would be the sound of a basketball that made me get out of bed along with feeling wet between my legs.

The night before, I had gotten into another argument with my William. The last time I was home for spring break, he said to me, "It feels different." I asked him what he was referring to. "Sex. You been with someone else?"

I was shocked and upset that, as I lay in bed, he would accuse me of sleeping with someone else. I remember trying to defend myself but he wasn't trying to hear me. That night in his room he questioned me and called me a lair. It was the first time in our two-year relationship that I felt verbally attacked by him. When I returned to school a few days later, he kept up his assaulting words. Even with tears streaming down my face and pleas in my voice, he didn't believe me.

"You gotta be doing it with somebody else. It doesn't feel the same. Who is it?"

"William, I swear I'm not messing with anybody up here."

"Then why is it when I call your room phone, you never answer? That's funny to me."

"Because it's midterms. Everyone is either handcuffed to a table in the common area studying or at a desk or table at the library. Me and my roommate go the library to study."

"Why can't you do it in the room? Why you gotta leave?"

"Because there's too many distractions in the room."

"Well, my homeboy told me his girlfriend goes to MCC and she doesn't study as much as you claim. Why you lyin'?"

"I'm not lyin', William. I am for real. I'm here taking five classes. It's not like MCC here."

It didn't matter that I was at a four year University and his homeboy's girlfriend was at a Community College which would result in different study habits between us two. It didn't matter that I gave him the exact reason why I wasn't in my room studying. Nothing I said changed his mind about me cheating. Finally reaching the end of my rope, I blew up on him. I told him I was over being yelled at and accused of something I wasn't doing. I remember talking to my cousin later that evening about his claims against my faithfulness to him. She said something I have never forgotten and would refer to when situations like the one with William would arise.

"If a man tells you the sex feels different and you know you're not doing anything, it means he's sleeping with someone else and she's turning him out."

I was hard-pressed to think that William would be cheating on me. He loved me. He cared for me. He wanted to wait until after I finished school to have a baby and get married, the order didn't matter to me as long as we did both.

Hanging up with her, I finished the conversation with my roommate. She, too, was having issues with her boyfriend which led to us spending the rest of that Friday night eating Domino's

Pizza and drinking Fruitopia. It was how we wound down before such a thing as girls' night out entered out lives.

I don't recall how long we stayed up, but the next morning I hopped out of bed because I felt something wet coming from between my legs. I was sure I hadn't urinated on myself. As I got up, I looked back at my sheets to find a small pool of fresh blood. Grabbing my shower caddy, and wrapping a towel around my waist, I hurried to the communal bathroom. In the single-person bathroom, just off our room, I pulled my night pants down to find blood clots in my panties. Then there was a smell that I had only experienced once before. It was the smell of life. I got the first scent of life when my nephew was born the year prior. Since him and that moment in the bathroom, I have never gotten that scent across my nose again.

I felt cramping as another blood clot dropped into the toilet. I silently cried in the bathroom, feeling my body vacate something I hadn't known I had inside of me. Following a shower, where I cried even more all alone, I went to the hospital to be examined. They confirmed that I had miscarried. As they asked me a series of questions, I answered that I hadn't thought about a missed period because I was focused on school. They assumed, based on my answers that I was no more than four to five weeks along.

Arriving back at my room, I told my roommate what happened and then called my mom. They both asked me if I was okay and supported me. The next call I had to make was to William. Because our call from the night before ended in me hanging up and yelling, "I hate you," before slamming the phone down, I wasn't sure if he would answer my call or not.
On the third ring he answered, "Yea?"

"Hi," I didn't know what to say.
How was I going to tell him about what I lost and that I hadn't even known I had it in my possession?

"Hey." He was short with me and I with him.
I could tell he was still on fire from the night before. Silence fell between us before he asked me what I wanted. With him

speaking with a full-on bad attitude, I knew that if we were to get through that moment, I had to remain calm. I didn't want to add more fuel to the fire that was still smoldering between us.

"I wanted to talk to you about something that happened. I had..." before I could finish, he interjected what he thought I was going to say.

"You cheated, didn't you?"

I don't know if time stopped or if I was just at a loss for words, but I couldn't speak or move. There I was, ready to share with him that what we'd made in love a few weeks ago had slipped away in the early morning hours and there he was accusing again. I wasn't in the mood to defend myself again, so I just blurted out, "I had a miscarriage today."

The silence returned after I heard him suck in the air around him. I continued to tell him all that happened that day and that I would be home in a in a few weeks. Just listening to me, he didn't say a word until I asked him to say something.

"I don't know what to say. What do you want me to say?"

"Nothing. I guess."

To be clear, he was not callous in his response. There was concern and care in his tone. The fire from the night before quickly lost its flame. On the other hand, the dead air between us was a signal that we had reached our max time together. Yet, I wanted to hold on to hope because after all, when he arrived, he had hope in his words, in his embrace, and in his love for me. I couldn't let him go despite the claims of cheating that he'd hurled my way. I didn't want to be single, unloved, and alone again. Experiencing him was life to me. I felt that without him, life would be over.

Surprisingly, he didn't want us to end either. Life wasn't over for us just yet. There was still room for hope to flourish, to try one more time at forever.

Spilled Hope

Weeks passed and we never talked about what we lost together. He would just ask me if I was okay and I'd ask him the same. I don't know if he was okay, but I really was not. Oddly, I couldn't tell him how sad I was at losing something so precious and wanted. Being able to tell him anything suddenly was not an option.

While I was at school, he had gotten a car. He and I were both excited about it because it meant we didn't have to bother my mom about using her car or bumming a ride from his cousin. When I returned home at the end of my sophomore year, I went back to work are KFC. One day I asked him if he could pick me up from home to take me to work. He refused, saying gas was too much to be driving everywhere. Not wanting to upset him, as he added that his aunt, who had two adult boys, kept asking him for a ride but wasn't paying for the trip, I had taken a taxi. It was my fault that I was running late because I had overslept that afternoon and missed my bus. But I'd been sure I could get a ride from my man. I know my mom would have dropped me off, but she wasn't home at that time.

At the end of my shift, tired from working, I called him and asked if he could pick me up and take me home. I had even offered gas money. Again, he declined to pick me up and gave some excuse as to why he couldn't. I ended up calling my cousin and paid him for the ride home. A taxi had more than a thirty minute wait for the next available pickup. I was too tired to wait. When I got home, I showered and went to bed.

The next few days I had hardly seen or heard from him. When I was able to reach him, it was for short moments of time. He kept telling me how busy he was and that he had picked up another job, which I hadn't known. Knowing he had a second job made sense as to why my calls went unanswered and were short. He was working to make his ends meet and to keep his car going, made sense to me. So, I didn't find fault when we would go days without talking to each other.

At that time, we were well into the summer and the days were longer than usual for me. I noticed pregnant bellies everywhere I went. It was like they stuck out like sore thumbs. I could hear a wailing baby a mile away and seeing my nephew made my empty womb jealous. One night while me and William were together, I asked him if he wanted to try for another baby. He told me no because he wasn't ready for a kid and that I didn't need one while in school. I reminded him of what he must have forgotten, only for him to say he wasn't trying then and didn't want to try at that time. I felt broken because I wanted to be a mom and coming as close as I had fueled that desire even more. Not trying to get me pregnant was a like a calculated feat for him. Right before he would climax, he would spill his seed on the bed or on me. I guess it was better to plant his seed on something that wouldn't bear fruit than to plant it in my fertile soil. Each time he did that, I became angry. Soon I stopped expressing my frustration and would rollover like it didn't matter what we did or how we did it. He made sure to leave his seed outside of me. I don't know how I held on so long, but as the summer ended and school was nearing, I had become extremely annoyed with him. I picked fights just because and lost sexual interest in him. Cheating was not an option, so I stopped initiating it with him. One morning, after spending the night together, while he was dropping me off at work, I told him that I didn't want to be in a relationship anymore.

He never looked at me as he drove, he just shrugged his shoulders and said, "You should have told me this earlier. You could have gotten a taxi to work."

As harsh as that was, as much as it pinched my heart, I didn't cry. I was literally drained of tears. All the nights lying next him and letting my pain roll down my eyes had emptied me out. Him dropping me off that day would be the last day I saw him. I left for school a few weeks later and that was it for us. Two years of love ended without a fight, a disagreement, or hateful words. His words are what made me fall for him. My lack of words made me fall out of love for him.

To Be Continued...Or Not

Time quickly moved my junior year of college. But not too fast for my heart to heal. I still loved William and wanted to know how he was fairing.

A month after I left for school, I called him. I was hoping he would be home because I wanted to see if he wanted to try for forever, again. After talking it over with my roommate, I had come up with a planned speech to present to him. I would take it all as my fault for not being a good woman to him and tell him how I wanted us to work because love was still present in my heart. Well, sadly, on the third ring, when my call was answered, it was not a baritone voice that I heard. It was a soft, feminine voice that greeted me.

"Hello," she sounded like she was either asleep or resting.

I looked at the receiver of my dorm room phone, I still didn't have a cellphone, and thought I had dialed the wrong number. I hadn't.

I asked, "Can I speak to William?" Hearing her voice caused a huge lump to form in my throat. It caught every bit of pain that wanted to spill out of my mouth and the pressure from that lump held back my tears at the same time.

"Who is this?" Whew. I cannot begin to explain the pricking pain that was in my heart. It was as if little cuts were being made with each passing second. I don't know how I made it through that call but I survived long enough to tell her who I was and to again ask for him to come on the line.

I asked him how he was doing to which he replied, "I'm good. Just lying down with my lady." I choked on his words as the lump tightened. I couldn't believe what I'd heard seep out of his mouth. We had only been apart for a month and he was already in a new relationship.

My hope in forever was gone. A new hope filled where I once was. Not only was the hope for forever gone, but it would never have a chance to come back around should the hope he had in her failed. He told me, and to this day I don't know why he said it, "Yea, we're having a baby too. She's going to have my first baby." Maybe she was urging him to say that, maybe not.

I don't remember if I said anything after his statement. I like to think that I congratulated the two of them, it makes me feel better thinking I had. We weren't on the phone too long before ending the call. When I hung up, I didn't look at my roommate, I just said, "He gotta baby on the way," then burst into tears. I believe the tears that flooded my bed when I lay down were struggling to come out when I first heard her voice. I cried myself to sleep wondering if I would ever love for real again. I wondered if I would ever be loved for real again. Tears streamed as my dreams invaded me, but they didn't bring hope, only doubt, failure, and fault.

Holding back my tears to keep him from hearing my anguish wasn't a hard thing to do. I had mastered hiding my feelings since I was a little girl, doing so as an adult wouldn't be any different. I later found out that he had a baby girl and had married her mother. The more of his life I found out about, the more tears formed in my heart, but nothing leaked out besides a little pain that I could manage. Years later, when we ran into each other by coincidence, we reconnected and began a fling. He told me that he and his wife had married but divorced two years afterwards. Reconnecting with him at first was a moment of time I had hoped for. I thought hope returned, I was wrong.

Between the last time I saw him and heard his voice, and the next time I saw him, life had changed him into a different man. Smoking and drinking had become a thing for him, none of that had been a thing for him when we were together. His choice of words were far different than what I was used to hearing come out of his mouth. He sounded like a sailor by the way he cussed, which seemed like every other word. He wasn't rude or disrespectful to me, I just wasn't attracted to the new man he had become. I could only assume life had taken the best out of him and only left what I had seen in those few months we were together again. To be honest, besides the sex, there was nothing of the new man that I wanted. We ended what could have been something again, never to revisit it.

The Measure of a Man

To give William credit, he became, prior to the last few months of our relationship, what I would measure every man I dated against. He set a standard that I desired and would feel let down when I did not select a man that measured up to the level of love and care he gave me. Between the end of our relationship to the beginning of the one with Christ, not one man made me feel like William did. With him I felt absolutely beautiful, wanted, needed, and desired. You couldn't tell me that I wasn't his main priority and that anything mattered to him outside out me.
The way he held me in his arms, I knew I was safe. It didn't matter what was going on around me, as long as he was there, nothing could get to me. Joking around, having laughing fits, going to my favorite place in the City, the Genesee River Falls, in the middle of the night were our things to do. Watching movies until the movies watched us would be how we ended many nights. Being left in his bed while he went to work, then being there when he returned was how I wanted to spend my life with him. William became what I knew as real love. It was felt in all my senses and would be a strong desire for years to come.

Spoken into Existence.

When I turned twenty nine years old, I gave my life to Christ. It was in the early months of being saved that I had to face what my heart had been holding onto for ten years, the loss of something I wanted more than life itself.

I remember my pastor preached a sermon on being upset, angry at God for something that occurred in our lives. As he spoke, I felt a tugging in the pit of my belly. I tried to ignore it, but it would not let up. At the end of the sermon, he welcomed people to the altar for prayer. He said that whatever God allowed to happen was for our own good. As he was speaking, the tugging became more intense and before I knew it, I was at the altar being altered by the word of God.

With my head hung low, I told God, as my pastor had instructed us to do before he prayed, that I was angry that I had lost the baby. I was hurt because I didn't know it was there and for all the years after I tried, He never allowed it to happen again. I was upset that many women around me had the pleasure of giving birth to children. I couldn't understand how something like that could be for my good. I was blinded to the goodness by the loss.

To add more to my sorrow, for those years prior, I felt it was also my fault that I lost my little bit of hope made with love. The night before I miscarried, my roommate and I talked bad about our boyfriends. I remember speaking into existence what I didn't want but wanted out of love, "I'm glad I didn't get pregnant by him. I hate him. I'm glad we don't have any connections. I'm done!"

The next morning, that connection was gone. I was never told that it wasn't my fault, nor did I ever tell someone how I felt about speaking the words of death over my unborn child. I carried that weight until the night of the prayer from my pastor. I wish I could remember word for word what he said. What I can reminisce on is him saying, "If you give it to God, whatever it is, He'll give it back to you." He went on to say how nothing God takes away, does He not plan to replace. For the most part, He would replace what was taken or lost. How was God to become my child? I had no idea. Part of me didn't accept what was said because I couldn't see how it would apply to me. But I gave Him my sorrow for the loss I suffered.

A few weeks later, at a conference at my church, a lady that had befriended me told me that many things could have caused the miscarriage. She said sometimes the body rejects it or it could have been something wrong with the child and my body knew it so... That did help a bit because it made me feel as if my words didn't cause the life that was growing to slip away. I know it may sound weird, but I would rather my words do less harm than my body. Yet, I felt my body was against me because it rejected something so precious.

I can laugh now at how I was thinking then. If it wasn't my mouth, it was my body that had caused much pain. I didn't really think it could have been a God-protection kind of thing for a while longer. When it did hit me that he was protecting my future and my womb, I just gave Him thanks, for I could have been a single mother raising a child without a father. The best part of understanding is knowing that I will never know what could have been, but I can believe what will be.

Trust God's Ways

Did you know that a lack of understanding of how God does things can wear you out? If you don't understand His ways you could end up fighting and resisting things, thinking they are an attack from the devil when they are an attempt by the Lord to work something good in your life.

Sometimes you may fail to realize that everything that feels bad to you is not necessarily bad for you. Reminding yourself that His ways are not your ways will help you trust Him even when your circumstances are hard to understand. As your day ends, just put yourself in the hands of Almighty God, and rest in the knowledge that He is good and knows what's best.

For my thoughts are not your thoughts, neither are your ways my ways, saith the Lord. For as the heavens are higher than the earth, so are my ways higher than your ways, and my thoughts than your thoughts.
Isaiah 55:8-9 ESV

Hope Lost

I once heard that your twenties are the times to try new things and explore all possibilities that life has to offer. So, I explored new cities, met new friends, got new jobs, new haircuts and styles. Lastly, of all the things that I could have a possibility in, I tried a new romantic relationship.

Jay appeared out of nowhere one day as I was walking home from the corner store. Crossing the parking lot at the beginning of my street, I heard the bass of loud music coming up behind me. Used to hearing it, I thought someone was just turning around in the parking lot. I learned I was wrong in my thoughts because as I turned around, I saw a car coming up behind me.

I screamed, "What the…" as I hopped out of the way. Even though I was more scared than angry, my words came across as such.

"Yo, you ain't gotta cuss me out!" The man in the passenger seat hollered through the driver side window as he leaned over the driver.

"Why are ya'll trying to hit me?"

"You didn't hear me calling you?"

I did hear a voice say, "Aye, you," but I didn't turn around. My mama told me that only street walkers turn when horns are blown or when men call out without using a name. To this day, I don't turn to honking horns or calls for my attention. I believe if you want my attention, come up to me. I guess because of my notion to ignore him, he decided to have his friend get my attention another way.

"My name not Aye."

"Whatever. You heard me."

Not in the mood to play with that negro, I returned to my walk toward home. My heart was pounding, and my attitude had turned up!

Moments later, "Yo, you just gon' walk away like I'm not trying to talk to you?"

With my attitude still intact, "If you wanna talk to me, get out the damn car."

And he did.

Walking from the passenger side door was a short, light bright skin toned man with a gold bottom tooth and a confident swag. I remember nothing that he said beyond wanting to walk me the rest of the way home and that he saw me walking when I left the store. His cousin drove up to my house after I told him I was just a few houses down.

The total opposite of what I physically liked—tall and black in skin tone—whatever he said was enough for me to give him my phone number. At that point in my life, I was still hopeful but annoyed with men. I don't know how that was possible, but I was. It was as if I wanted one around but didn't at the same time. I mean, I enjoyed the company of a man but I didn't want to enjoy the company of a man. I don't know if it makes sense to you, but it does to me.

Well, Jay was different than the two priors.

Wait, here is what I literally just realized as I am writing about him: back then, men didn't have to do much to get my phone number. I just freely gave what should have been worked for, and that goes beyond just my phone number. I can only assume that my need to feel and be loved caused me to give away myself just for the 'fix' I needed. But to God be all the glory that I only had to give myself to Him one time and forever does He supply my 'fix' for love.

By saying Jay was different, I mean, he was a working street dude. I know that sounds confusing but let me explain just in case you don't get it. He worked a parttime job as a line cook at a local restaurant and sold drugs on the side. I can only guess money on the job was not enough, so he had to do what was needed to make ends meet. Smoking and drinking was his choice of relaxation. For him, partying was life and life was a party. I tried to keep up with him but could not. The only time we saw each other was at night. He worked during the day just as I did. After six p.m. it was just us. I don't even recall how we started dating, but we were for about seven months.

During that time, I had tried over and over to become pregnant. He said he wanted me to have his baby and I wanted to do just that. I had one close, wanted call, but only one line appeared on the stick.

Pause for the cause: I was destructive as a young woman. I can believe…I can believe…I can believe the things I did for love and to have a child. But God. But God.

I didn't care if he would be there for the me and the baby, I just wanted his DNA to help me to create what I wanted. With him, I did not feel like I felt with William. I felt like an afterthought most times because he would forget to come see me or keep a date that he asked for. Making me a priority wasn't going to happen. I fit in behind his job, his other job, his friends, and his new son. I don't know what order they all fell in, but I was after the last one on his list. I could have been lower for all I knew at that time. Accepting the unacceptable was what I did to keep myself thinking I was wanted and loved.

I remember when his birthday came around, we planned to go out to the club with a few of his friends to celebrate him. He told me he was getting a rental car and that he would pick me up on the night we were to go out.

Dressed and excited to be going out on the town, I waited for ten p.m. to roll around. I texted him to see if he was coming and was told yes. So, I waited a little while longer before texting him again. That time, my message went unanswered. I tried calling but was sent to voicemail. The crazy part is that the phone he was using was in my name. He needed a phone, I had great credit, so...you know.

Well, to no one's surprise but mine, he didn't come get me. In fact, it would be days before I heard or saw him. When he finally came around, he said he'd forgotten about me and that because of all the shots of alcohol he couldn't drive home. The entire phone call sounded of full of lies and excuses. He never told me why he had taken so long to answer my calls and messages. That question was skipped over with, "Yo, I was just...you know." No, I did not know but didn't express how I felt. For years, it didn't matter so why say anything?

Two months later, my birthday rolled around. November 14th of every year is a national holiday and I celebrated as if it were. That year I had turned twenty-three and had a small party at my house. I had drinks, food and a table for spade playing. I turned the upstairs attic into a little juke joint for the night. A few friends and cousins packed the upstairs and we hung out for hours. Jay and his brother arrived two hours after it started. He played a few hands of spades before saying he needed to leave. Promising he would come back, he left never to return that night. I kept calling and texting, and again my messages and attempts to reach him went unanswered. The night ended with me alone, wondering what I had done wrong to make him leave on my special night. I never did get an answer when I asked what happened.

He just said, "I had work."

While dating him, I felt like I was alone most of the time. Thinking about it now, I realize we never really did anything outside of my house. When I asked him about meeting his mom and sister, he said he would introduce me to his sister but not his mom. According to him, she didn't like meeting new people. I was his girlfriend not some random "new people." He said she still loved his son's mother and that it would be an issue to introduce me to her at that time. I don't know why I was okay with his reasoning, but I was. I understood what he never said: I wasn't good enough to meet his mother let alone to be seen with him off my street. Even on his days off, we only did things under the cover of darkness.

Pause, again: Do you think I was sane during this time? I don't. I was still searching for love and it didn't matter how I got it. I didn't even really love myself. I just tolerated me.

When I say we never left my street, we never left. At that time, I never wondered why because I was just okay with having a boyfriend that wanted a baby just as much as I did. Granted, he'd recently had a baby birthed, but it wasn't from me, so it didn't matter much.

I can't help but notice the selfishness in my heart at that time. Jesus, thank You for being a womb protector! I wanted a family and did not care who I made it with…even if the father was not ideal.

Well, just after Christmas, when tax season came around, suddenly things changed. This time I couldn't take it. Like William, Jay had gotten a new truck and his disappearance became too often for me not to say anything. Yet, I held back because, "I got work," was going to be the excuse and why bother my soul? To the credit of him, he didn't have to hide anything because I wasn't looking, but the truth of his life was about to hit me hard.

One afternoon, me and my older sister got into an argument. During the screaming and yelling, she blurted out, "That's why Jay got a girlfriend and a baby!"

I didn't know what being hit with a stack of bricks felt like before that moment, but I can tell you now that it hurts like all hell.

The lump that had formed in my throat when I heard William's new lady answer his phone returned! It was larger than before.

I could only get out, "What?"

She repeated it again with even more poisonous venom. With each breath I took, my chest felt like it was collapsing on me. I felt tears welling up in my eyes but the lump in my throat had swollen to the point that it closed my tear ducts.

To add to the strain of hearing her words, my cousin said, "I was going to say something, but I saw him with her. They live over on Avenue D. I didn't want to say anything because it wasn't my business."

Do you know what being hit a second time with a stack of bricks feels like?

I'm sorry to tell you, but it is death to the soul.

I stood there while they talked about what they knew and saw my man do with his girlfriend. I wanted to run. I wanted to hide. I wanted to sink into the concrete ground that I stood on. As they spoke, everything from the prior seven months flooded my thoughts like a broken dam. Everything he said, every excuse, every, "I got work," suddenly made sense.

I assume there is no need for me to go back over it all, but the point of no return arrived, and I crossed over into it. I called him, told him what was revealed to me. He tried to defend himself by stating, "That's not my baby. She was pregnant when I met her. I just claimed the baby as mine." His lies fell on a broken heart, they slipped into the abyss of I don't care. I ended our relationship by handing up and immediately disconnecting the phone he had. I didn't even cry myself to sleep that night.

What I am learning now is that it was that night that seeds of bitterness had been planted in my heart. The only thing is that the germination process would take years before the root began to grow and the tree began to spring forth.

But before I could move on from Jay, there was one last seed that needed to be planted by life.

I received a call just after Valentine's Day that confused the heck out of me. Answering my cellphone, I heard, "Bi*ch!" then a dial tone when it ended. The number was a blocked one so I couldn't call back. A few minutes later, another call from a blocked number. I answered it to a woman asking my name. I told her and she asked me who I was.

Confused I said, "I'm Ebony. Who is this?"

She didn't answer, instead she proceeded to tell me that she was Jay's girlfriend. She wanted to know everything and without hesitation I told her. She told me that she worked at night as a nurse and that was how he was able to be with me. She was with him on his birthday and confirmed what he said about the baby not being his. She told me that he wasn't there when she had the baby and wondered why he was with me while she had her baby. As we spoke, she then asked me if my sister was such. I told her she was and then she wanted to know if my sister had known about me and Jay being that my sister and her mother were friends. Not wanting my sister to get into trouble with her friend, I lied. My sister was the one that told me, not to be a protector of her little sister, but to hurt me. And it worked.

At the conclusion of our call, he had arrived at her home. He started yelling at her about me. I heard him call me a lair and say that, "I wouldn't eff with no fat girl!" I hung up when I heard those words. I was over men denying me in front of others, particularly in front of other women. I was over being hidden like I was someone to be embarrassed about. Sadly, it would not be the last time I allowed myself to be hidden. I had become used to it to the point that if we were in public, I was sure it had to be a fluke in the time matrix.

Hope is for the hopeless. I had a lot less hope when my twenties began to turn into thirty. But before I crossed over into a new decade, I had no hope at all and the last hope of the decade.

No Hope at All

At twenty-five, I was determined not to fall in love with men, again. I kept them close enough for me to be pleased but far enough away to keep feelings in check. It wasn't hard to have no feelings for any man after dating Jay. I had become emotionally unavailable to them in the romantic area of my life. If a man wanted to be my friend, he would get the best friend in me. If he wanted to be more than that, I wished him well and sent him on his way. The soil of my heart had hardened. From what I could tell, based on my actions towards men, it would take a very patient man to till the ground of my hardened heart.

JK was introduced to me by my sister's best guy friend. It was not a, "Hey, you two should link up," but just a normal introduction when someone new comes around. Our first interaction was of us being spade partners, which we lost to my sister and her best friend. After that first day, we became friends. He was a cool guy that liked to smoke and chill, doing whatever made him happy, including me.

For me, happiness was whatever the day brought me. It didn't matter if I wanted what the day offered, I felt I had no choice but to take it. I had reached a point of not knowing what happiness was when I decided to play a man's game and keep my emotions to myself when dating them. I only wanted what I wanted and nothing more, certainly nothing less. If a guy could not supply my needs, which were not much, I would turn into

Casper the Friendly Ghost and disappear without rhyme or reason.

For a few years I was in a situation-ship with a guy that was younger than me. JK, as I called him, was three years younger than me at twenty-five. Our connection was strictly sexual. We didn't look for chemistry between us, no. We looked for the attraction that led to my bedroom and hotels many times throughout our five years sprint.

JK was a very cool and laid-back man. He was smooth in his approach to me and I liked it. He was the second guy whose body I enjoyed very much, William was the first. I knew in the emotionless arena of my heart that nothing could come from us being together, but that didn't stop me from enjoying his company. He was the only man, at that time, to meet my dad. Actually, he and William were the only men to shake my dad's hand. I remember when they first met. JK and I drove around the city one afternoon doing nothing in particular when my dad called me. He asked me to come by to see him, which I did. Pulling up to his apartment, I got out of the car and hugged him.
Hugging me back, he leaned over the drive side door and demanded, "Aye, nigga. Get out the car. Let me see you."
Unbuckling his seatbelt, JK did what my dad said. "My bad, man."

"Yea. Let me see you." My dad stood taller and bigger than JK and I think it intimidated him a bit. Folding his arms across his chest, he looked JK up and down then said, "What's your name, nigga?"

Leaning against my car, at first he stood up and extended his hand for a shake. "JK."

"Uh. What kind of name is JK?"

"It's my nickname."
He snickered and when he did, I became nervous. I don't know why I had but I did. I wanted to get out of there quickly, leaving JK right there. Even now while writing this, I don't know what I was nervous about. I didn't think my dad was going to swing on him, but something wasn't settled within me. My dad stared at him for a few minutes before I broke the awkward silence that

had creeped up between the three of us. I asked my dad what he was up to and as we talked, JK went to get back in the car, but he didn't get far.

"Where you goin', nigga?"

"Back in the car."

"Nah. My daughter not in her car, so you don't get it in. Come back over here let me look at you, nigga."
Again, doing what my dad said, he moved back to the side of my car.

"Dad, stop. Please." Thinking about it a bit more, I recall how he grilled William when we were dating. It was quick but my dad just asked a few questions and left it alone. I wasn't sure if him grilling JK was going to be good because we were not in a relationship nor leaning toward one. I didn't want my dad to scare him off from me. But now, as an older adult, I wish I would have allowed my dad to grill every man that I dated. I believe he saw something that I didn't see or that I chose not to see.

"Nah, Ebony. I just wanna know the nigga datin' my daughter."
I stood back quietly as he asked JK, "You got kids, nigga?"

"Yes, sir. Two. A boy and a girl."

"Wouldn't you wanna know the nigga datin' you daughter?"
He rubbed the nape of his neck in a nervous move as he answered, "Yes."

"Good."
JK darted his eyes at me then back at my dad. That look meant he wanted to get out of there. I didn't blame him because I did too.

"What's your plan with my daughter? You ridin' in her car. What's your plan?"

He looked over at me and before he could say anything, my dad said, "Don't look at her. Look at me."
Writing this, I have a smile on my face and tears in my eyes. I hadn't realized until now that my daddy was protecting me in the only way that he knew how. At twenty-eight, I didn't appreciate

the protection, now at thirty-eight and no longer having my dad, I appreciate the protection. I wish now more than ever, I could have him vet men for me. This late in life, still desiring to married and have children, I wish I could have my dad grill the man I would marry beforehand. Maybe he could see something I may not be able to. That is one loss I will have forever. Now, I must lean on God to guide me and be my protector as I date.

My dad bossed him around so much that day that he just did what my dad told him, again with an answer to his question. "We're not dating. We're just friends."

"Just friends, uh? That is all you plan to do while ridin' in her car? Where your car at?"

Before JK could answer, I stepped in. "Dad, we're heading out." JK hurried to the passenger side of the car, got in, snapped his seatbelt, and got back in his comfortable position. I said goodbye to my dad just as he said, "You ain't gon' say bye, little nigga."

I slipped into the driver seat when JK leaned over to say his goodbyes to my dad.

"A'ight, little nigga. Take care of my daughter."

"A'ight."

I shook my head, waved at my dad, then pulled off. Approaching the corner of the street, I looked back at my dad through the sideview mirror. He was still looking at us drive away. I wish I would have known then what I know now. Maybe I would have allowed the grilling to continue. Maybe waiting three years before he met my dad would have made me rethink being with a guy for only sex. Maybe if I would have built a solid, trustworthy, father-daughter relationship with my dad, I would have avoided the pain prior and the pain to come. Maybe just before falling for a man, I would let my dad do the vetting.

Taking his opinion as the protection it would have been, I could have chosen wiser then and now. It's funny how we can learn something in our youth that we don't find valuable until adulthood. I wish I would have gone back, turned around, replayed that day, rewound, and let JK answer my dad's invasive questions that were meant to protect me. I see know that my dad was showing me the type, the caliber of man that I hand in my car, in my life, in my body. But I can't go back. That time is gone forever. There is no going back. No replay. Life moved on. And now, in my life without "The Griller of Man", I am uncovered. I am exposed. Now what?

Turning the corner, I apologized for what my dad did. "I didn't know he was going to do that."
He said it was cool as he understood why he questioned him. We enjoyed the rest of our day and ended our night wrapped in my sheets.

For five years, we maintained an off and on-again friends with benefits relationship. He was the only man I was slept with during that time. I wasn't particularly sexually attracted to any other man. The times where we were "off" he, on the other hand, was "on" with someone else. One time, after a few months' hiatus, he told me he had another baby on the way. It made me sad because I wanted a baby but couldn't get pregnant to save my life. Without doing anything to prevent it, I felt okay to give him a baby for my sake. But it never happened.

It was being with JK that made me set in my heart that I was barren. I felt that way because he was able to have a baby with someone else but not with me. Since it had been just short of ten years since the miscarriage, I was confident in my self-diagnoses that I was unable to have a kid, or at least carry one to term.

Although what me and JK had was not a relationship in the normal sense, we did have a friendship that was important to me. It was such because without it, I wouldn't have been able to see the protector in my dad rise and do what it was supposed to do. I wouldn't have known what it looked like for a dad to protect his baby girl. Plus, JK would be the first guy I had sex with after becoming saved and entering a covenant with Christ. I'll talk later about how that happened and what the effects of it were.

All the chambers of my heart lost hope expect one. In it was the last hope and it would come in the oddest of ways for me.

Last Hope

During a time when me and JK were "off", I heard about the online dating website BlackPeopleMeet.com. Viewing the photos of the potential matches, I signed up for a free account, created my profile and swiped left until I saw and read what was appealing to me. I thought by searching online, I would yield better results than the men that resided in my city. I widened my criteria to one hundred miles or more from Rochester. I felt that if I was going to meet someone, the farther away from the streets of the city he was, the better. I was convinced, through my own tainted eyes, that there were not any good men in my city and that they must be in others.

Setting up my account, I began to send flirts and winks to random men from as far away as California and as close as NYC. I chatted with a few that flirted back but didn't exchange numbers. Some men seemed to be ready to knock on my door and start a new life. I wasn't that ready for that but honestly, I was tired of being alone. I hated attending family functions alone and attending group dinners as a single friend. I wanted a man by my side to fill the void that feeling unloved and emotionally scarred left behind. I remember sifting through hundreds of men's photos in search of what, I had no idea, but I was sure to know it when I saw it. One thing I knew for sure I didn't want was a man that had kids. I preferred, and still do, men without children. Except now, as I am much older than when I searched for love online, I find that many men in my age group have children. So, I adjusted my preference to no more than two kids. More than that and I don't even consider the man as an option.

Well, when I came across Duke's page, it was not by chance. He sent me a flirt followed by a message. I had no idea what I would get into by replying to a simple, "Hey, beautiful." But I was all for it.

Duke wasn't from the same city as me. He lived all the way in NC. Meeting him in the summer of 2011 made him my last bit of hope before God swooped in to renew it. I remember that while using the site for free you couldn't exchange phone numbers. The system was set to find nine numerical digits in conversations and would delete the message if found. Cleverly, he sent me his number spelled out for some numbers and the others numerical.

The first call we had, we talked about how smart he was for thinking of how to get me his number seeing that neither wanted to pay for the membership. We shared what it was we did for work/career, where we lived, and what we did when we weren't working. What drew me to him was that he was a creative like myself and had dreams and goals that he was actively working toward. He attracted me to men who knew and operated in their purpose. I didn't fall for him right away because I was still in a bad emotional state with loneliness and the desire for love and to be loved. But I liked him. He was funny, interesting, and charming.

The months we had taken to get to know each other were filled with long hours spent on the phone, over a few hundred text messages a day, and a rising desire to let down my guards to let him in. By the end of fall, we had begun talking about what we wanted for the future...together. To go after his dream of becoming an actor, he was preparing to move to Atlanta and wanted me to come with him. Without hesitation, no discussion needed, barely preparing for something of that magnitude, I agreed to leave my life in Rochester to support the life he wanted in a new city.

Pause for the Cause: I now understand why God tells me to get out of my feelings. When I 'feel' something, I move toward what I feel instead of what I know. I honestly get it and understand it now. God doesn't operate in feelings, He is logical. My feelings told me to move with a man I had fallen for, had never met in person, with a limited history, and a future of only potential to offer me thus far. Instead of being led by what I knew, I was being sold a dream, a hope that was clearly shown on my sleeve, a lack of security and a filler for my loneliness. Note to self: remove my feelings. Grab ahold of logic.

I was filled with new possibilities of a marriage, family, the cure to my loneliness and fear of dying alone without children. He gave me a renewed hope in the words and plans he had made for himself that now included me. He told me to look for a house, not an apartment, for us to live in that cost between $200k - $400k, so I did. I searched all over the Atlanta area, found house after house after house. I just knew that all was going to be well, and I had finally been found in hope with love.

I prepared to leave by looking for call center positions in the new city I would be living in with my man. I wanted to help pay the bills too, to make sure he didn't have to carry the financial burden alone. He told me that he would move first, then I was to follow three months later. He was a man with a plan and I was a part of it.

I remember my best friend asking me, "What does he do for a living that he can afford a $400k house?"
I told her, "He's an actor."

Now, I know that sounds foolish, but I genuinely believed in him and in what he said to me. I wanted to believe in the unbelievable moments in life. I wanted to believe that I was worthy of a man that wanted to do life with me, weaved me into his future, and wanted to build with me. To my ears, I heard no lies, no selling of an empty dream. I didn't heard a rock that would break a promise neither the opening of Pandora's box of destruction. I heard none of it.

One…Just in Case

I could hope in him, dream a new reality and plan for it, but I couldn't put all my eggs in one basket. I had learned that when I gave my basket of eggs to a man, he would return it in worse shape than when it was given to him. Eggs would be broken open, cracked to the point of leakage, or missing. Many times, I had to repair the handle on the basket with duct tape or twine. The more I did, the weaker it became. It began to lose its integrity so much that I had to be incredibly careful when carrying it. I couldn't swing the basket and when handing it off, I had to tell the man, "Don't carry it by the handle alone. You have to support the bottom."

The bottom of my egg basket was just as bad, but it held together. Nothing dropped out from the bottom, but the sides were a different story. There were rips and tears that I tried to stitch together with more duct tape and twine, but it would not hold for very long. A few times my eggs would slip out. Some I was able to catch, while others hit the ground never to be used. My heart is the basket. Hope for a husband, love, care, support, belief, future planning, hope for children, hope for a family, fulfillment, desire, need and want were my eggs. During my journey of love and relationships, I lost many an egg. By the time Duke arrived, all I had remaining was hope for a husband, children, and a family. The worse part was that I only wanted the marriage to have the children. After the children were born, it wouldn't have mattered if he remained or not. History says I could do it alone and be successful at it.

For my twenty-ninth birthday, that year of meeting Duke, I went to New Orleans for the first time with one of my homegirls. We had an amazing time during our four-day stay. On the first day and night there, I fell in love with the people, sight, sounds, food, drinks, and atmosphere of that beautiful city. And on the second day, I fell into lust of this fine police officer mooning lighting as armed security for a nightclub. I saw him as my friend and I walked down Bourbon Street doing nothing but enjoying ourselves. I remember locking eyes with him, smiling, and continuing to walk.

Then I heard, "You're just going to keep walking?" Laughing, I turned around and nodded my head. He yelled, back, "Okay then."

We strolled the street until we noticed the crowd was thinning out. Heading back the way we had come, we entered a few of the bars to get a shot or two…or some before hitting the street again. By the time we reached the bar he was securing, I had enough liquid courage in me to stick my tongue out at him in a teasing manner. He responded by telling us to come into the bar. After giving him my ID, he said, "I'm keeping this just in case you get out of hand and I have to take you in."

"Take me in?" It was then that he flashed me his badge. I tried to snatch my ID back, but he moved his hand before I could.

"Look, you make this hard, I'll haul you off right now."
I stood looking at him and smiled, "Fine. Keep it. I just need it before I leave on Sunday."

"Good. Ebony Nicole Smith."
I giggled and headed into the bar. There was a live band playing, which is what made me start loving live music from that very moment. At the counter we ordered more shots and enjoyed the music. As the night rolled on, we left to hit the streets searching for food. Not far from the bar I heard my name being called out. Turning around, I saw him sprinting toward us. I had totally forgotten about my ID. Handing it to me, he told me to put his phone number in my phone and to call him later. I didn't know what later meant, but I added his number to my phone and me and my friend found another bar that sold pizza. Getting couple of slices, we ate and chatted.

It would be late morning when I sent him a message to remind him of who I was. He said he hadn't forgotten and was waiting for me to contact him. He told me that he was at work and would reach out later, which he did. We met up for a late lunch and it was then that he told me he would be in Buffalo NY in January and wanted to make sure we linked up. I was all for it, of course.

To sum up the weekend, my birthday was amazing. I was not ready to go back home by far but had no choice. I spoke to Duke throughout the weekend who told me to be on my best behavior. I promised him that I would and was. The last night of the trip, the officer and I made plans for him to come back to my room. But for some reason, not even noticing, my phone had been turned to silent which meant I didn't get any of his messages that followed. I returned to my room. It was a moment that was missed.

When I landed back home, I sent Duke a text to let him know and was told to call later which I had planned to. My cousin picked me up from the airport. I was telling him about the trip and how much fun New Orleans was and about the officer I had met. As I was talking to him, I looked down at my phone to see I had dialed Duke. The time on the phone that counted the length of the call was already six-minutes in. My mouth dropped and I hung up. I told my cousin what happened and he laughed. I knew Duke had heard everything that was said and when he called me right back, I could hear the hurt in his voice.

He didn't yell at me, he only asked that I call him back when I reached home. I don't know why he didn't go off on me like someone else would have. I couldn't wrap my head around what he heard and how he responded. I thought for sure he would have blown up on me, I know I would have done it.

I was so afraid to call him back that day. He kept texting me telling me not forget, but I would just reply that I would not. It would take hours later before I dialed his number to hear what he had to say after I explained myself. He told me he heard the entire conversation because of the accidental dialing of his number. He said he was hurt because he wanted to ask me to be his girlfriend, who I assumed I was, seeing as though we were planning a life together in another city.

After sharing his heart with me, I apologized and told him I wouldn't call the guy. He wasn't happy with that and replied, "He has your number so he can still call you."

"What do you want me to do? I can tell him not to reach out to me again when he does call."

"No. I want you to change your phone number. Now."

To secure my new relationship, I changed my phone number the next day. I had called AT&T, got the new number, and he was the first person I called after the change. He was okay with it and we moved on to building our relationship.

I also had a backup plan when it came to my basket. Although I carried twelve eggs, I would always keep one for myself before handing it to a man to carry. It was just in case he broke the entire basket, dropping all the eggs and destroying everything. If he did that I would not be left empty. Although, out of fear of missing my last hope, I gave him every egg except one. Love.

Losing the Last of Hope

As the year ended, Duke and I planned for him to come to Rochester to spend a couple of weeks with me before heading to Atlanta. I was excited because it meant that I would not spend Christmas alone that year. The plan was for his cousin, a truck driver, to bring him as far as Philly then I would drive six-hours to pick him up. I didn't want to drive alone so my mom and sister came with me. We met in the parking lot of an Ikea at 3 a.m. on a Monday morning. When I saw the truck, I hopped out of my car, excited to finally see him.

It was a moment that was seven months in the making. We embraced and kissed. I met his cousin who then left to finish his route to NYC. After meeting my mom and sister for the first time, he was hugged and welcomed by them both. Soon, we were back on the road to Rochester. He drove because I had driven there and could not turn around and do another six-hours. The ride was filled with laugher for the first few hours, then silence as the three of us went to sleep. Once we reached home, he showered and climbed into bed with me.

Wave the Flags

A few things came to light while he was with me those two weeks.

I'm a cuddler, he was not. The first night he was with me, he rejected me hugging him. His exact words were, "Ugh. Don't touch me. I don't like to be touched when I'm sleep." His back was to me and every night we slept that way.

One night, I was cooking dinner for us and he was in the kitchen with me as I did. I don't remember what I ate but when I tried to kiss him, he rejected my kiss. He put his hand up to block my lips from touching his. It hurt, but it was my fault because my breath wasn't smelling too good from the ranch-flavored potato chips.

We had dinner with my best friend, whom I'd told everything he had said to me. I told her about the plans for marriage, children, and moving. She asked him, "What are you plans for her?" I was happy she asked because I wanted him to confirm what he'd said to me. To my dismay, he told her he didn't feel like he needed to tell her his plans for me. I was crushed. Everything he'd said, I wanted my best friend to hear because she, at times, did not believe me.

I remember leaving him at the restaurant we'd gone to so that we could watch the football game. I'd left him there to bring her home since she lived near the restaurant. I told him to call me when he was ready. Arriving at her apartment, I cried because I felt like he should have answered her. I felt that since he knew how important family and friends were to me then he would be happy to show my friend that he had good intentions when it came to me, but he did not.

When Christmas arrived, he did not have a gift for me, but I had one for him. He said he spent all his money getting to Rochester and that that was my gift. I accepted it.

Every year my family spends the holiday together. For him, it was not ideal. He stayed seated on the steps that led to the second floor of my aunt's house. While we were enjoying each other, he was off to the side, texting on his phone…or whatever he did. Later that evening while heading back to my apartment, he said that he doesn't like family gatherings and that when we had our own family we would celebrate with just us.

On social media, he would make subliminal messages that I felt were directed toward me and my family. He told me that I was being sensitive and that if what he posted bothered me, then I should unfollow him. He would also comment on a few of my friend's posts, but never mine. When I did comment on his posts, he would text me to remove it, so I did. Other times he would just ignore my comment.

I guess I had to see the red flags that were flying but I failed to pay attention. Everything I wanted to do, enjoyed doing, he rejected. I knew I would have to adjust to his way to become his wife and build a family. The funny thing is that when I brought him to workday to meet my work friends, one of my close friends told me, "Eb, I don't trust him. He has shifty eyes. He doesn't look people in the eye. I do not trust him."

I wish I would have paid attention to her warning.
Duke was scheduled to leave a few days before the New Year for Atlanta. I thought he had secured his ticket to get there, but he had not. That man had no way to get from Rochester NY to Atlanta GA. And I had no way to get him there. He told me again that he spent all his money to come see me. Thinking about it now, if that was the case, he didn't have as much money as he claimed. In the end, I had to humble myself and ask family and friends for the money to send him to Atlanta. I could not scrape up the money at all.

I told him to try asking family and friends on his end. He said he wouldn't do that because it was my idea for him to come to spend the holiday with me. Since he was right in his statement, I didn't fight it. I just kept trying. Every option was failing. Down to none, he called his friend who said he would loan me the money to send him to Atlanta. I agreed to borrow the money, buy the train ticket, and repay his friend when I got paid the next week.

Pause for the cause: I had to pray for the silly twenty-nine year old woman that did anything to be loved. I apologized to her for accepting the unacceptable just to feel accepted. I should have had more hope in myself. I think if I had, I would have avoided much of what I allowed to happen.

The day he left, I was relieved because I really did feel like I was stuck. He didn't want to do anything with my family and only wanted to stay in the house because of the cold. The odd Facebook messages continued and whenever I said something about it, he would blow me off and call me sensitive. I chose to ignore the posts and just prepare for the move to Atlanta.

The True Pursuit of Me

On December 31, 2011, I became a saved woman of God. I don't know what I was doing, but the week prior, all I wanted to do was go to church. It was the first time I had ever felt that way. I was invited to my co-worker's church service that Saturday night. I hadn't planned on being prayed over, becoming a servant of Christ, or joining the church all in a matter of minutes. But there I was, a new woman on the last night of the year.

My new pastor told me, "God is about to change your life."

That new change, which I had to spend a couple of years getting used to, came with a change I was not expecting.

The next morning, the first thing I said was, "I'm saved. Now what?"

When Duke told me his plans for Atlanta, it included him living with his female friend that was an RN. I had spoken to her few times on the phone and had no reserve about their friendship. What I was not expecting was the sudden shift in communication between us. We went from talking and texting every day for hours on end to a few messages a day. Many of my messages were ignored or answered with one to three words. When he did return my calls, he asked me twenty questions that I had to answer then he would tell me, "I'll call you back." That call wouldn't come for another three to four days.

In between, I was still calling just to get his voicemail or texting with no response. For me, it was all rejection, but I held on to hope. I thought he was working, which is what he said. He told me he had the chance to audition for a Tyler Perry play and was focused on his lines. I understood the focus because I was focused when I had written my first book. I had to support him from where I was and that meant understanding he could not fool around with me on the phone like we used to.

The change in our relationship birthed a bit of insecurity in me. I remember he posted a picture of his friend, saying about how proud of her he was for passing an exam. I *liked* the post and left a congratulatory message underneath it. Something in me told me it was more than what I saw, but I ignored my feelings.

Three months later, in the middle of the sermon, my new pastor stopped preaching and said, "I don't know who this for, but God is trying to get you out of that relationship. He is no good for you. Let him go."

His words hit me like a brick and I lowered my head and cried. I knew he was talking to me, I just didn't want to believe it. I was in the last bit of hope for my forever. If I didn't make it work with him, then my plan to marry and have children would be washed away. As much as I wanted to not think about what my pastor said, I couldn't help it. I kept replaying in my mind all that Duke and I had gone through since I had become saved. The lack of respect, communication, and the rudeness in his social media posts began to add up very quickly. In my hearts of heart, I knew I could not continue with him.

I remember later that night, I called Duke and told him I no longer wanted the relationship. He didn't seem bothered by it at all. He told me I could do whatever I wanted, and I did. I tossed and turned all night long, asking God if He was sure I was supposed to break up with him. At that time, I didn't know the voice of God, so I didn't hear anything besides my sniffles and all hope going, trickling down my face onto my pillow.

I was alone, again. No hope left.

I held on tightly to the egg, which kept me alive. Love. Nothing else mattered after losing Duke. My heart began to feel differently. My thoughts changed and I was okay with it. The way I was hopefully thinking was getting me nowhere fast.

With just the love I had hoped to receive one day, I followed Christ. Along the way He told me, "You are a wife. You are a mother. You will give your husband three children, two boys and one girl." That was in the summer of 2012. At the time, this memoir is being penned, it is 2021. I am yet unmarried, and my womb has yet to be filled with life again. But God is so good and faithful that He prepared me for what He said. He had to first teach me how to clearly hear Him above all things. And He used what He knew I would be drawn to, to do it.

Father, forgive me for my complaint against the waiting I am in. I know I am waiting, not in vain, but in You. I am waiting on Your love that is incomparable to any other. I am waiting on Your grace. I am waiting as I am being sharpened into the woman You created me to be. Yet, I become sadden by what I see that others have what I desire. I know this is my journey and there will be no one to travel it beside me.

Father, I ask that You Help me with being okay with this wait. I know I must and I will, but I don't want to be like the children of Israel who wanted a king because everyone else had one. You gave them what they wanted when all they needed was You. I just want You plus other things. Help me to be okay with not having the other things now. Help me. Help me. Help me. Help me. I'm alone but not lonely. I can call someone to fill that void, but I don't want just anybody because I'm not just any woman.

Thank You for hearing me. For giving me the strength for this important season of waiting. Thank you for not giving me what I want just because it's what others have. Thank you for keeping me covered and closed off so that not just any man will see and find me. Thank you for answering my request. I count it done and to be seen when you deem it and me ready. I love You from now until my very last breath.

Here I Am

Here I am standing tall despite the baggage I've had to carry. Here I am walking in my purpose. Here I am, flying high when those below me tried to clip my wings. Here I am breathing when fear had its grip on my throat. Here I am living when death knocked on my door, but Jesus rebuked it when He answered. Here I am, living in the shadow of the Most High when the world attempted to overshadow His glory. Here I am with The Great I Am. I know not where these next days, weeks, years, and seasons will lead or bring me, yet, because I know He will never leave me, is for me, and is keeping me, I'll be just fine. Although I cry and want to lie down and die, here I am still going. Here I am. There you are. With Him we stand.

Amen

Section Three: Massive Heart Attack

If you feel heart attack symptoms: Do not delay in getting help. Do not drive yourself to the hospital. Do not dismiss what you feel. Women tend to have symptoms more often when resting, or even when asleep, than men do. Emotional stress can play a role in triggering heart attack symptoms in women.

Lord, I Heard You Clearly

I wasn't looking for anyone. I wasn't ready to date. I wasn't interested in being in a relationship at all. I was simply happy to get to know Jesus. There was a zeal about Him that I had, and it kept me focused on Him and only Him. Whenever the church doors were opened, I was there. If there was a revival or something happening in other churches, I was there.

I remember having notebooks filled with the teachings my Pastor gave and with what struck a chord with me. My pastor would often tell us, "Go home and read it for yourself," and I did just that. It was what kept me in the bible after bible study on Thursdays and after service on Saturdays.

It was during that focused time with God that He said, in the summer of 2012, "You are a mother. You are a wife. You will give your husband three children: two boys and one girl." To-date, nine years at the time of this writing, have passed since He spoke that promise to me. He also said to me in 2013 that I would meet my husband that summer.

I only recall one other time hearing of His voice and it was when I was car shopping and wanted to purchase a BMW that was ten years old. I remember hearing a voice tell me, "Purchase the car. You will have it for three years." I wish I were well aware of Him at that point because it would have saved me three years of car notes. Nevertheless, He spoke to me and I had to learn to believe in what I heard.

When God told me I would meet my husband the second year of being saved, I didn't know what to do. I wasn't sure who he was, when and where he would come along, or how to tell if it was him over someone else. I never did ask God to help me to know, I just thought, being a new babe in Christ, that I would just know.

I did not.

The funny thing is, I met two men that summer. One indirectly and the other directly. To explain it as simple as I can without pushing ahead of the story, one would become the source of the last ounce of water to cause the Tree of Bitterness, as I call it, to spring forth. While the other would be the first time I experienced a soul-tie being broken. Neither were ideal for me. Yet, God needed them to break me from my past and to heal the WHOLE woman.

To be honest, looking back over it all, I'm glad He did what He did and how He chose to do it. I'll tell you why in a while. I hope you will understand how much He loved me and loves me to do what was essential for my mental, spiritual, and emotional growth.

Did You Hear That, For Real?

As hard as I try, being able to remember years past, I cannot recall how John and I met. The first memory I have of him was me visiting his office and us chatting about the book publishing and magazine publishing business. He did the latter. I was very intrigued by his southern charm. He was firm in his speech but caring in his choice of words. There was something about him that was different than what I was used to, which drew me in. Again, moth to a flame, I was googly eyed when I talked to him. I saw no fault in the man that stood before me. Perfect, no, but perfect for me, yes. It would be years of dancing around each other, losing touch, coming back together for a publishing project for feelings to resurface with a mighty force.

John was a cool and collected man. Nothing seemed to rattle him except the women he chose to date. I remember he would tell me how this one did that and the other did this. I never asked him what he did to get the responses from the women that he received. I just believed it was their fault. I mean, I, like him, had been a victim of love in the hands of the wrong people. I felt the need to save his broken heart. I knew I could show him how a man like him should be treated. I was confident that by showing him differently, he would see me and all the hurt from yesterday would disappear because the love from me would encompass him and just fix what they had broken. I was so sure of it.

We spent time together to reintroduce ourselves to each other. I had fallen in love with the man he had become between 2014 and 2016. He was a breath of fresh air and I was happy to be able to breathe, again. I was confident that after getting to know him and he me, he would see that I was what he needed in his life. John was a man, mans and in that was where I felt protected. When he wrapped his arms around me, I felt like nothing—same as with William—could harm me. I loved hearing his voice over the phone, and I loved how when we saw each other, his face would light up. I remember leaving my job in the middle of the day to spend the afternoon at his office. Being an entrepreneur awarded him freedom during the time of day when most would be working, but we would be doing everything except working.

The day John and I decided to cross the line from friends to more than was on Super Bowl Sunday in 2017. I knew what calling him earlier that day to have him come to me after the game would lead to. I knew what I wanted, and I wanted it from him. He would become the third man I had chosen to sleep with since becoming saved. Three and a half years had passed between the prior man and him. So, for me to find him worthy of my body was something I didn't take lightly and neither did he.

That first night was so sweet. He came over, we chatted and then the night moved according to how I had hoped. The next day, I called off from work because I wanted to spend that day with him. He left that morning then came back that afternoon. In my mind, sadly, I thought for sure we would be heading toward a relationship.

I was wrong.

Following the night we first shared together, I felt bad about what happened because I had entered into a convent with Christ after having sex in 2014. The convent I entered stipulated that I wouldn't have sex until I was married and that I was worth the wait. That night, I removed my ring because I knew that what I was about to do was wrong, but I ignored my feelings and let the lust and hope I had lead me. It wasn't anything he had done, it was my denial of what I'd heard from God.

Two weeks before the night he and I had shifted our friendship, God said to me. "Daughter, walk away from him." I heard Him, clearly, but shook my head, "Lord, why?"

"He's going to try to destroy you. Walk away now!"

"Lord, not him. That's not what he's going to do. He loves me. We talked about getting married and having a family. He wants a daughter. I can give that to him."

"Daughter, this will not turn out well for you. Trust me, walk away."

I ignored my King. I shut Him out of my love life. I didn't want nor need His help to get that man, I was able to do it on my own. From that moment on, I didn't hear God on anything John and I had done. Without God, our feelings for each other were moving along at a fast pace and that renewed my hope that I had finally been found. As I told God, we had talked about a family, marriage, and what we needed from each other. He was everything I had hoped for, a protector, a provider, he loved me, he wanted marriage and children. One thing he didn't have, however, was a relationship with Jesus.

I remember he asked me as we laid on my sofa, "Why do you always talk about Jesus?"

"Do I?"

"Yes," he laughed, getting up from the place where we were relaxing. He walked towards the bathroom, looked back at me, and laughed before heading down the hallway.

When he closed the door, I thought to myself, Maybe, I'm being too Holy for worldly good? It was then that I decided not to talk about Jesus too much around him, I decided that if it made him annoyed with me, then I wouldn't do it anymore. Besides, I had a bunch of Holy Roller friends I could talk to about Jesus. They loved Him as much if not more than me. Whenever something he and I conversed about could relate to the bible, I would just make up a lie...

Pause for the cause: I would make up a lie to keep the conversation going between us. I would say how someone I knew experienced the same thing and how they solved their issue. I couldn't give him the word of God which would have helped him better than a lie would have. I was causing my own damage and didn't realize it.

Then There Was None

Being divorced after twenty years of marriage and not having children for his legacy, John, I just knew, was going to have me at the altar in no time. He was eleven years older than me which made me believe that the age difference would cause all games to be tossed out of the window. I was sure he would follow through on the words he'd spoken to me months prior. However, a few months after we made the shift, he was no longer sure if he wanted to get married or if he even wanted children. The more I walked toward marriage, the more John dragged his feet.

The conversations about marriage all but ended as I tried to hold on with my whole life for the possibility that I still believed in. However, there would be one conversation that threw everything into a spinning fan. I had allowed months of frustration and confusion to build up beneath the surface of my heart. When

I finally let it out, not in a rude or destructive way, telling him how I felt, he blew up on me.

I tried to calm him down before it became worse than what I thought it would be, but the damage was spreading as fast as a wildfire. He told me I was being selfish for not understanding how he'd been feeling for the last few months, feelings that I knew nothing of. Apparently, he'd been dealing with a few issues privately and felt that I should've understood that he was struggling. I tried to sympathize with him, tired to offer my help, but nothing I offered or said would calm the fire that I'd started. From there, things changed for the worse. Our conversations, which I would initiate, turned into short phone calls and messages with two worded answers. "I'm good." "Oh." "Cool." "Good for you." The good morning, good afternoon, and good evening messages stopped. The pop ups to my home ceased too. Mentally, I was losing it. I couldn't understand how someone who wanted to love me, who wanted to get married and build a family with me, could all of a sudden turn his back on me. It didn't make sense to me because I loved him and he'd said the same. I'd placed all the hope I thought I had left in him. What was I going to do?

Trying to reach him, to smooth over the damage I'd caused wasn't working. To keep him, I had to just toss away my ideas of marriage and accept a basic relationship. Because he changed his mind about marrying me, I had to be okay with only being his girlfriend. Even then, I didn't feel like he really wanted me. That was unacceptable, I had to make it right. I had to get him back to a place of loving me, of seeing a future with me. If he didn't, then I would be out of luck, out of hope, out of time, because I was thirty-four and once I crossed the line into thirty-five, I would be in the high risk zone for birthing issues. He was literally the final straw.

Pause for the cause: As I write this, my heart beats free of the hurt that once caused it. The residue of pain has been healed. I don't know how I survived it all, but I did. I wasn't hearing God concerning him anymore, so I had no idea what to do. I was too ashamed to even pray about it since it was my decision to not walk away when God said to do just that.

The Rise of a Standard

I asked God to set the **standard** for which I could measure a man. I've never had a healthy male in my life that I could measure another man against as far as dating or any other reasons for a man to be in my life. I believe that a father sets the **standard** for his daughter, a standard that if a man doesn't meet or exceed, then she should not waste her time. So, when I asked God for the **standard,** the first thing that hit me was Jeremiah 29:11.

The plans. God has plans for me. See, with this He set it so that if a man doesn't have a plan for me in his life, then he is just winging it to see where it goes. A plan is a vision as well. In Proverbs 29:18, the bible says, "Where there is no vision, the people perish: but he that keepeth the law, happy is he". If that man doesn't have a vision, a plan for us, then I'm not the one he's looking for. God has a plan and a vision for my life and all I have to do is take His lead and not lean on my own understanding as to where He is leading me.

A plan. A man must have a plan for me. Plan a date. Plan some time alone. Plan to call. Plan to stop by for a few hours out of the day. Plan a trip. Plan a nice afternoon together. Plan. Plan. Plan. "I know the plans I have for you, declares the Lord. Plans of good and not evil to bring you to an expected ending."

What's the ending he plans to have with you? Is it temporary or for life? Is it to be his girlfriend or his wife? Is it to string you along for a few years or within a year make you his wife?

Section Four: Recovery Time

In general, heart disease treatment in women and in men are similar. It can include medications, angioplasty and stenting, or coronary bypass surgery. Cardiac rehabilitation can improve health and aid recovery from heart disease. Angioplasty and stenting, commonly used treatments for heart attack, work for both men and women. But for coronary bypass surgery, women are more likely than men to have complications.

I don't recall to whom this was written nor when it was written. It was an email I found a while back. I saved what I had sent because I was re-encouraged by my own words.

Woman, you may not know much about Who He is, just as I didn't, but take this day, Easter, as proof of what He can do.

See, for three years He schooled people on the Word of God, taught His crew how to hold it down once He left. He was snitched on by one of His boys and was jumped and murdered by haters. And those that He thought were His best friends left Him when it all went down. But, His Daddy is an old school G!

He put His Son to sleep for 3 days so He could heal from what happened to Him. He knew J had more work to do and needed strength and power to do it. J rested and when He got up He did so with all the power He would need to keep you from the same fate two thousand years later. He had changed so much that the crew He rolled with didn't even recognize Him. He had to prove Who He was just to get them to believe He had changed and had come back. They all counted Him out. But the way His life is set up...

The point is this, yes life is tough when you have to work, lead, dodge haters, get hurt by them, and still do things you don't want to but have to do. Yes, it is exhausting but I can tell you there is no greater rest than the rest in Jesus!

He said we can come to Him and He'll give us the relief we need. He'll exchange our pain for His joy. Your haters won't know what to do with you and those you know might not either. Some will fall away and some will stay. But it's all okay. Don't look at what you lost, look at what you gained when you relax in Jesus, the power to do anything impossible!

Easter isn't about candy and cute dresses. It's about a Man that loved you so much that He set provisions before you were born. It's about knowing you don't have to run in cliques, clubs, and gangs to feel like you belong somewhere. It's about acknowledging you are important enough to live and die for.

It's about Christ Jesus!

(John 17-21; Matthew 11:28; Isaiah 43:1-7)

The Path of Pain

There is peace in singleness if you know how to get it. There is a peace that keeps you focused on the promise and less on the problem. It's indescribable, enlightening, and encouraging. It's freely given, yet hard to obtain. So, how did I, a woman that dated men just for their seeds, end up peacefully single?

I gave up!

Seriously. I gave up trying to be seen, heard, and understood. I gave up trying to be what I thought a man would want me to be. I gave up trying to be who I thought I needed to be to be chosen by a man as his wife. I gave up on finding a man to love me. I gave up the option of being a single mother. I gave up the jealous emotion I would feel while watching other women around me enter into relationships, get a ring, marry their best friends, and have children. I gave up my hope to obtain the dream and the desire in my heart.

I gave up trying to figure it out on my own. I gave up trying to hurry God along. I gave up on getting my hopes up whenever a guy wanted to explore the possibility of a relationship with me. I gave up the drive to be the first girl in my family to get married. I gave up trying to be the first to get married and then to have children. I gave up on all of my back up plans that would come into play if marriage and children didn't happen by forty, plans that included creating my family alone via adoption or IVF.

I gave up trying to survive heartbreaks, let downs, and broken promises to myself. I gave up questioning myself, gave up trying to figure out whether or not I was good enough for a good man. I gave up any and everything a good man had to offer.
I let it all go.
I gave it all up.

I had reached a point where I was overworked by my thoughts. Aging according to a clock that I'd heard ticking since I turned thirty years old kept me in a whirlwind of worry. There were days I would be okay with aging, with growing older, which put me at risk of not having children. Then there were days I would soak in my sorrow as the desire for a family seemed to increase with every new year that arrived. The more I thought about all that could happen, the more I almost drowned in the sea of loss possibilities, the more I lost hope.

My view of relationships and marriage had changed for the better, but before that could happen, I had to be restored. The restoration would take almost two years to be completed. Although there are still some things that need to be addressed, the whole woman that is Ebony Nicole has been restored. God had to take me through the valley to get me to the river that flows with mike and honey. While in the valley, I felt alone and confused as to why love had treated me so badly. I felt as though all that I had hoped to be, a wife and a mother, had been swept away with the time I felt I'd lost.

I remember being at such a low, dark place and not caring about a man and his feelings. There was this guy named D that wouldn't let up on trying to date me. I was very rude to him, tried to push him away by playing games that I knew would lead to him being hurt. Well, one day, during a text conversation, he wanted to make plans for us to go out that weekend. Just as I was responding, I heard a voice say, "Raise his hopes and crush his dreams." I closed out the message, deleted the thread, and blocked him. As much as I could have done what the voice recommended, I refused to be the cause of someone else's pain, refused to be the reason why they felt negative toward women.

I remember sitting at my desk and quietly saying, "Lord, help me."

That was in the early part of 2018. In those moments of texting him, I was okay to inflict some sort of emotional pain, the same kind of pain that I had been dealt. It would have only been right for me to pass it along, to allow someone else to feel how I felt, to make them question God, question themselves, to give up like I had. Ninety-seven percent of my heart was blocked due to the trauma I had experienced for so long. Yet, there was this small three percent that gave me room to breathe, room for blood to still flow. That was enough for me to change my mind about how I was ready to destroy him.

I had no hope for my heart nor for anything that came out of it. I remember telling one of my friends that I had put up a guard to protect my heart. I explained to her that I had built a concrete fortress with sharp shooters on every side, cannons ready to go off, a moat of water with spikes just beneath the surface of the water. I had the draw bridge up and a hard, wooden door that had a steel frame behind it so that if someone thought they could get through the wood, they would be surprised at the steel behind it.

I was determined to make sure nothing could penetrate my heart again. I wasn't going to die another love death. I had just enough love to give to my family and friends and that was it. I wasn't going to jeopardize that love for the sake of a man. All of me was, again, off limits to men. If a guy wanted to do business, needed me to join a project, wanted my input on something he was working on, I was all in. If he wanted to chat about a book he wanted to write, I was all in. But if a man wanted to date and get to know me, he wasn't going to get far. I had shut down everything around dating and that shut down had become my only form of protection. I was once exposed, then I built my fortress and there my heart was safe, protected, and guarded by the walls that I constructed.

What I didn't realize was that while I was busy keeping everyone out, I had inadvertently kept God out as well. My friend and I were talking and, after I explained the purpose of my fortress and the protection I had around it, she asked me one question that caused me to tear it all down.

"So, how would God get in? Guards can't keep God out, but with all of that protection you can."

I couldn't say anything to answer her. I thought I had God in my heart, which I did. But the one area in which He needed to be, I had kicked Him out too. I had given God everything except for the love and hope I had for marriage and a family. It was my last bit of hope for the future and I was determined to hold on to it. I didn't want to let God in because nothing seemed possible when it came to love. It didn't make sense to give to Him what I couldn't seem to hold on to. The love I had received, accepted, was what I thought I was worthy of. Since my reality proved it to be true, there was no need to give God my truth since He already knew it.

As much as I wanted to keep doing what I was used to doing when it came to protecting myself, I was failing. Fast and hard. He, being so kind and loving toward me, would take the time to show and tell me what it meant to be loved and how to do so properly.

I just had to remember the promise made to me long ago.

Get That Name, Have the Baby, Then Leave

Be as honest with yourself as I am with you as you answer this question: Do you or did you want the wedding more than the marriage?

While you think about it, be truthful with yourself and answer the question with the true contents of your heart. I'll share my response: YES! I wanted the wedding more than the marriage. I've planned that day so well over the years that when it comes time for me to actually do it, all I've have to do is choose one of three wedding coordinators that I've wanted to work with. The idea of the wedding didn't include anything that he may or may not want because it would be my day instead of our day. Can somebody say, "Selfish"?

I know. It was where my mind was. I just wanted to feel special, beautiful, and finally loved correctly by a man. In my early twenties, the moment after saying "I do", dancing in the middle of the dance floor for the first time, and leaving at the end of the reception to start our life was as far as my imagination went. I didn't think about the first week, the first month, the first ten years after that night.

The thought of what to do when or if things fell apart never entered my mind. How to handle arguments weren't a concern of mine. Wondering what to do if he required me to do something I didn't want to didn't worry me either. I had a mental limit on marriage and it wasn't worth much. That limit wasn't even close to how marriage could really be. It wouldn't be until my early thirties that I would begin to think beyond the single day in our life that would make use one forever.

At twenty-five years old, for some reason, I had a change of heart when it came to marriage. For a long while, although I day-dreamed and planned my wedding, I wasn't too excited about the marriage. I thought that if I married then I would lose who I was and my own identity. Along with that, having to ask for permission to do something or to go somewhere bothered me. I couldn't understand why I needed to ask a man if I could live the life I loved or what his opinion was about something.

I was so used to seeing men come in and go out of the lives of those around me that the benefit of having one on a permanent basis wasn't anywhere in my line of vision. I saw them come around, blend in with the family, share a few laughs, attend family functions, smile for the pictures, and then just as quickly as they arrived they would be gone. It would usually end when it came out that the woman he was with had become pregnant or for some other reason unknown to me.

Not only was this how it was in others' lives, but in mine as well. You read the stories about the seven that loved me and left me. I couldn't see the point of marriage to a man. They never seemed to stay around long enough to be considered for it. I can only be honest with you because I'm being so with myself. I swear, men, in my eyes, had only one purpose. Making babies. Oh, and having a boo-thang to take pictures with.

Funny part, I don't have any photos of me and my exes. Not a single one. As I record the truth of my past, I had to stop and cry and pray. I don't know why I don't have photos of us or anything that remained outside of flashes of memories. It saddens me somewhat because I feel like the more time passes the more they all fade into the blackness of my memory.

I wanted to marry someone, get his last name, and start a family. It wasn't about him or what he wanted or needed. I didn't care. I was so used to pouring everything into a boyfriend only to be left empty that the mere thought of pouring into a husband seemed pointless.

I wanted the wedding and children!

The only reason I wanted a man was to make babies. For as long as I can remember, I always wanted to be a mom. Growing up around single mothers and becoming friends with others that were, I was confident that I could have a baby and raise it/them on my own. I'd seen it done for so long by so many women that it didn't seem too bad of an idea. As you already know, I did try to become pregnant after it happened when I was nineteen years old. You know how that ended. But it never happened again. Because my trying yielded zero results, I assumed I wasn't able to have any children. That was when I changed to dating men with children, hoping their kids would fill the void I had. That didn't work either.

Men are very protective of their kids, odd way of finding that out seeing that it wasn't that way with me and my dad. I honestly can't remember meeting any of my exes kids except one, and it was clear that his kid would always come before me.

A quick memory: this guy I was dating picked me up from work one afternoon. As I approached the front passenger door of his car, he let down the back passenger door and said, "Get in the back."

I peeked in the front and didn't see anyone until I got in. It was then that I saw his son, around the age of seven years old, sitting in the front seat. I didn't say anything like, "Put him in the back," because I wanted him to keep liking me, so I dealt with it. Looking back, I should have said something. I should have let him know that as a twenty-year-old woman, I wasn't going to ride in the back while a child rode in the front. But I didn't. I wanted to be liked then loved too badly to stir up any trouble.

Because I didn't understand the importance of having a man in the house, which one would think I would seeing as though I didn't have my dad, I lacked the understanding of the value of him. I saw a man for one reason and one alone. Give me babies.

I had a very unhealthy view of men and relationships, mainly men in the marriage relationship.

Then, at the age of twenty-five, something changed, a switch flipped on in my perception of men and marriage. I went from wanting one for only a baby and superficial reasons to wanting a loving, caring, and safe home built on a marriage. How did this happen? Where did this sudden change come from? To this day, I can only assume it was God changing my heart to prepare me for something I didn't know I needed, something beyond my wants.
The family I never had.

I didn't think I could become the woman someone could or would want to marry. I had too many failed relationships to support my thoughts. As far as I were concerned, I was correct. Only three men in my entire life discussed marriage to me but not with me. There's a difference. Talking about a plan for your own life doesn't automatically include the one you're having the conversation with. Seeing as though neither man asked me to be his wife, I was assured that my assumptions were correct. I wasn't wife material; I was only fit to be a girlfriend…if that much.
But God.

When He said to me, "You are a wife. You are a mother. You will give your husband three children, two boys and one girl," it was then that I became a wife and no longer a girlfriend. I was becoming someone's good thing, the reason why he would obtain favor from God, a helpmeet, the missing rib from his chest, the one that I would submit to, respect, obey and follow. Yet, at the point of writing this book, eight-years have passed without a man to marry me.

Was it too late or was I still in preparation mode? Looking back over the years, I see that I was still being prepared for my role as wife to one man and the mother of that man's children.

The Path to Healing

I had an idea of what love and marriage was, but clearly I was wrong. I knew for sure I was wrong because God surely wiped everything I thought I knew and understood about it away. He did what I call, blank slated me. The easiest way for me to explain it is as this:

Remember in school how the teacher had the blackboard that he/she had written on with white or colored chalk? Then at the end of class he/she would wipe it clean and sometimes would use a wet cloth to ensure it was cleaned for the next teacher and class. That's what God did to me. The thoughts stuck in my head were completely removed. I mean, I had not one idea of what relationships and marriage was supposed to be like any longer. He really removed it all.

My ideas of marriage focused on the love, relationship, and connection seen on The Cosby Show. What drew me to love the first black family of television was their ability to have an issue and have it solved in twenty two minutes of television programing. It was seeing the children have a father that was attentive to their needs and showering them with love, affection, discipline, and kindness. It was having a mother that was the same, but with more sassiness. The relationship of the grandparents to the grandchildren and the siblings towards each other was perfect for me as well. Everyone, as they grew, became successful with their own families, families that mimicked that of how they were raised. They had a healthy and loving relationship and that became what I needed and desired for my own family.

I remember daydreaming about a husband who was my best friend, my biggest supporter, and that never treated me as if I didn't matter. We would grow and build a life that was different from what I was used to, not that life was seriously bad because it wasn't. My mother did the best she could and for that, I love her more than my own life.

What I wanted, however, was a marriage where there weren't issues that would cause use to fuss and fight, issues that wouldn't have him leaving the home for a few days or for good. I wanted a marriage where we could disagree but do so respectfully and at the end, come to the best conclusion for our marriage and for our family. Through all, I had learned through television that I hadn't known the truth. That reality of marriage was non-existent in my immediate sphere of influence. It was the lack thereof that never challenged my belief.

Not leaving me blank and to be filled with foolish ideas, God taught me what it meant to be a wife and how one should conduct herself. I wasn't sure how to be a wife after losing the ideas I had. To teach me, God allowed me to notice more and more married women that seemed at peace and that were respected by their husbands. To me, those women walked and spoke differently. They didn't speak ill of their husbands, they spoke positive, good things about marriage. And even when they shared the bad, it wasn't in a way that made me feel afraid of marriage. It made me feel prepared for the "good and bad," times that were sure to come during a marriage.

So, how did I keep my mind from dragging me to the land of "It's too late,"? It was because of the wife He sent to watch over me as He watched over her.
Her name is Vanessa, and ever since 2014 she's been the wife I needed to see in order to become, by way of hearing, what a wife is.

Let me tell you about this amazing woman of God that was sent to be my earthly shepherd into wifehood.

She Was There All Along

God will always have a ram in the bush just for me. I believe this because as He began to remold me according to His plan for my life, He used my friend as an aid to His work.

I remember the day I felt as though I was running out of time to marry and have children, I was thirty years old. Crazy thought, right? I know it is. But for me, it was my truth. I'd been single for the last five years without a prospect in sight! So, how could I not be correct? Reality showed me that what I was thinking wasn't a lie. When I looked around and couldn't find a soul that wanted to build a relationship that led to marriage, that told me that I must've been correct. See, I had calculated time and it wasn't on my side.

"Okay, if we meet this year, then that means we have two years to fall in love and for him to see me as his wife, for him to buy a ring and then ask me. Then we have a year to plan the wedding and get married. It's recommended that a new couple should wait two years before having kids so they can enjoy their marriage with just the two of them. So that will leave us trying in the third year to get pregnant. But what if there are complications and/or miscarriages? It might take longer if issues arise. So, I'll add another year before we have kids. Add that up, I'll be married at 33 and a mom at 37. But they say after thirty five years old, birth defects increase." (Insert a wave of fear from every angle of life.)

Can you see how time wasn't on my side?

I was sure that if I could get just one man to dedicate himself to me, then I could hurry us along and become what I wanted and do what I desired. I didn't care who he was, where he was coming from or going. I didn't care if he would leave me after having his babies. Heck, I was raised in a family of single mothers and had many friends that were such. It wasn't like I didn't have ample examples on how to be a single mother.

I was on a mission during the first year of my thirties to be found and married in the timeline I had set. In those first twelve months, it didn't happen. So, I pushed it back another year, and another and a few more until my thirty fifth birthday. I won't go too deep into what we had because I talked about him already. I listened to what he was saying and fell in love with his words. That was the biggest mistake I had made and learned that mistake the hard way. His words were never followed up with actions that would lead to where I wanted to go and to what he spoke about. One move of, "We need to talk," and it was over. The dream he sold me, the hope I purchased fizzled away in the course of one phone call. By the end of the week, we had a white smoke rising between us which meant the fire was out!

Being at such a low place, I felt like all hope was lost concerning my dating and married life. I felt like having a child was out of reach for me as my thirty sixth birthday rolled around. All of my fears that had settled in his arms were resurrected when everything with him fell apart.

What I didn't know was that the road I was on already had a guide to my right side caught in the thicket. She had gone before me to pave the way for my arrival. I just didn't notice her. Like Abraham, when God told him to go Moriah and sacrifice his only son, she had already learned the way of a wife through trial and error. Just as he was going to do what God said, at the end of the road he found the help he needed to follow through with God's plan and instruction.

And Abraham lifted up his eyes and looked, and behold, behind him was a ram, caught in a thicket by his horns. And Abraham went and took the ram and offered it up as a burnt offering instead of his son.
Gen 22:13 ESV

I can't recall the exact way we became friends or how we even began to speak to each other, but years before I would need her wisdom, Vanessa M.F. was already in my corner, already my friend. A wife, a mother, a pastor, and greatest of all, a mentor to me, she proved to be just what I needed.

Before she had become a mother, and long before she had become a wife, she was a single woman enjoying her singleness. She wasn't worried about a husband because the influences of husbands around her failed to show her what a husband was supposed to look like. With dominating women in her life, the husbands were left powerless as putty. However, those strong domineering traits that ran through her family somehow didn't attach itself to her.

She remained a woman that was strong yet able to submit to a man that loved the Lord, would love her as the Lord did, and could lead her. She was confident in who she was which helped her gather and keep the nerve to dismiss any man she felt wasn't up to her standards. Vanessa was a young woman who knew who she was, who she wasn't, what she wanted and what she didn't want. And if she felt a bit of disrespect from anyone, then it was a wrap for them!

One thing she said about her husband was that he was a clubber when they met, but she wasn't. "He said he had to get himself together and couldn't play around with me because he knew I wasn't like the other women. He knew I was different without me having to tell him." Unlike my mentor, I felt I that had to tell every man who I was and tried to make him see it, foolish girl at heart.

Vanessa was truly a Ruth in her time. She lived her life on purpose and while living she was found doing just that. Living. She wasn't gossiping with her girls about when Boaz was coming or how much time she had before it ran out. She traveled, opened businesses, earned degrees, and served the Lord with her whole heart. She lived the single life she was teaching me about. She wasn't just blowing smoke, she taught me from experience.

It was her experience that God used to change my heart and mind about a time frame that wasn't His. As if playing a game of Spades, instead of hiding her hand from me, she revealed it. It was seeing what she was holding that showed me how to play the game too. It was because of her that I was able to get the healing therapy that I desperately needed. God used her in my recovery, but before He could, I had to be open and honest with the matters of my heart.

I remember sharing with her how bitter my heart had become from years of neglectful relationships that I'd chosen to be in. Years of feeling unworthy and loveless left me wondering if I were ever enough. I used to beat myself up when things went wrong, doubted my ability to be loved, to love, and to be so just for me. It was as if everything I did in my relationships was my fault and led to them ending. And if I'm honest with myself, in this delicate moment, space, frame of mind, I don't think I was ever myself with either of them except Terry. As I said prior, he was the only man to make feel beautiful and truly loved. It was him that I measured other men against, yet still accepted the lack that came from them not measuring up.

That is until Vanessa said, "You are enough. They just couldn't hold you in their hands."

"What do you mean?" I asked her for clarity because I really didn't get it.

Her response was, "Some men don't have big enough hands to hold you so they drop you or let you down. You are more than enough."

That was the first time I heard that I was enough, let alone more than enough. What she went on to teach me over the course of three years—yes, it was a long process—was how to love, cherish, and appreciate myself. She taught me how to look in the mirror and see what God created and how to see that it was good (Gen. 1:26 ESV). Vanessa opened my heart to the fact that God truly had my best interest at heart and that as long as I remembered Who He was and who I am, there was nothing that could change my mind (Psalms 139 ESV).

I praise You because I am fearfully and wonderfully made; Your works are wonderful; I know that full well.
Psalms 139 vs.14 (ESV)

I, Ebony Nicole, was wonderfully made from love and care and made to be more precious than rubies (Proverbs 3:15 ESV). Vanessa told me that in order for me to be found in love, with love, and for love, I had to change my perspective of myself, my perspective of love itself, and my relationship with God.
"Perspective comes when you grow in God and have built up enough maturity and spiritual muscle to look at life's challenges not only as tragedies, traumas, and bad breaks, but also when you're able to look deeper at the issue or situations and see the silver lining or see behind the scenes of the turn of events."
– Vanessa M.F.
I thought for sure that my past would haunt me to death and be the reason for my past and future failed relationships. I never knew it was my perspective the whole time. Go figure. All I had to do was see it from a different vantage point to get the wisdom and understanding that I needed.

Soon after talking with her, I was on my journey of change. I did this by seeking the depth of who I am and through prayer and self-reflection, a different perspective began to emerge. I started to see how God protected me in each occurrence and sought to learn the lessons I had failed to gather when they ended. Perspective was the cure I needed for the damage that had been done. I grew in perspective as it grew in me. Reality was truth but it wasn't my destiny. I had the say so in how those relationships would affect me. With a heavy heart and a sincere desire to be healed from my past, I allowed God to work on me.

Armed with nothing but hope and a willingness to be better, I continued to seek God and Vanessa for guidance. Whenever something would arise that God was working on within me, I called her. She would give me her perspective, back it up with scripture, and end that call with a prayer. An example of this was when God started digging up my past sexual abuses. I had long ago dealt with them, or so I thought. But not to God! She told me that He was breaking the curse that became attached to me from the abuse so that it didn't land on my daughter(s). I guess He broke the generational curse with her too, when he kept her from being like those who raised her.

Won't He do it?

In those moments with Vanessa where she poured her wisdom into this rebuilt, secured vessel, I learned to let go of everything that tried to kill me and to embrace everything that loves me. I stopped worrying about when my husband would find me, when my womb would be filled, and when I would hold the proof that he and I had been fruitful.

The change in my perspective has allowed me to focus on what I do have instead of what I don't. I have a great family and friend base, a budding business as a writing coach and a publisher, and a newfound love for myself. I use #CoachGottaCrush every Wednesday when I share a photo or more of myself and speak of me as though I am my own #WCW (Woman Crush Wednesday).

Honestly, I love the woman staring back at me in the mirror. Is she perfect? No. Does she have many flaws, faults, and failures? Yes. But none of that compares to the perfect, flawless, faultless and unfailing God she serves.

If it wasn't for the teachings of my mentor, Vanessa M.F., on how my perspective cures my view of men and relationships, I would still be the wounded woman that I was before her wisdom. It saved me and gave me a power I didn't know I had. The power to walk away from a man that doesn't see my value and worth without me having to tell him.

And if that is all that perspective does, it has done enough.

From a Heap of Clay to a Masterpiece

What do you see when you gaze upon your reflection in the mirror? Do you see what was created to give Him praise? Or do you see a heap of clay? Before He began to do a good work in you, you sat in the corner wet with tears, bent out of shape from carrying the weight of your past, poked by people who wanted to see what would come out of you. They saw a brown, mud-like substance taking away the beauty of things that were already completed.

But the Potter saw something greater, a reflection of His image. He saw His greatest creation. He looked at you, wet with the blessing He rained down from the windows of heaven. He saw you, pliable and ready to be used by Him, ready to be shaped into His purpose for you. He marveled at your brownness, knowing you would soon change once consumed by His fire.

The Potter knew He wanted you to be unique in all your splendid beauty. Should you crack due to mishandling, you're still priceless to Him. You'll simply be *Beautifully Flawed*. There's no comparing His work to others for His is crafted by hand, not by a machine.

The Twins

Often times, we look to the world for answers to problems the world has caused. Yet, if we only look to the Word for the world's issues, we would then find the answer. Jesus said, "In the world, you will have tribulation but take heart for I have overcome the world." Since we will, are, and have faced trouble, we will have, do have, and have had the answer right before our eyes.

See, God is not attracted to our problems, He is attracted to our praise. That is where He abides for that is what He said. He said He abides in the praise of His people. Whatever you face, Woman of God, believe He is with you, know He is working it all out for the good of you, and trust that He will be just what He promised. Once you get to a place where you can unlearn the ways of the world and learn the ways of the Word, life's battles will be seen as muscle builders and endurance testers.

What I love knowing is that grace and mercy are behind us. They push us to the next level. When we feel stuck, it is grace and mercy pulling us free.

The Key to It All

"Then they cried to the Lord in their trouble, and he saved them from their distress. He sent out his word and healed them; he rescued them from the grave."
Ps. 107:19-20 NIV

I can say that love feels different when you're loved correctly. For me, I'm secure in all areas of my life. I feel and know I am protected. I'm made to be comfortable with sharing matters of my heart even if they make the other person upset. I think before I speak because I don't want to destroy them with my words. Being loved properly makes me think differently. I believe in the person because hope in the person resides in my heart.

Thinking back again as I have done many times while writing my memoir, I realize that I wasn't supposed to know what love felt like with a man after William. I wonder if experiencing what it wasn't gave me the passage to know what it felt like coming from God. I wonder because God and Terry's love, although drastically different, were the standards of difference between Godly love and manly love. I hope that makes sense. It's like I have experienced man's love on one hand and God's love on the other. It would be thirteen years from one love to the next. Everything in between wasn't like the first nor the last love.

I can only hope and desire that the man God has for me will love me like Jesus' while being a man about how he loves me.

To further explain, Jesus loves me unconditionally, unrestrictedly, and with kindness. He speaks to me with kindness and when needed with firm authority. He doesn't talk down to me or make me feel as if loving me is difficult. Jesus leads me with compassion and provides security to the point where I am comfortable following Him. Likewise, William loved me for me. Even with my flaws, he was nice to me and didn't use the faults of my actions against me. He showed me how to love myself in the skin that I'm in. He taught me that it was okay to share my feelings and that they mattered. Simply put, with all of his own flaws, he still taught me to be myself while he loved me as myself.

It's No Longer Worth the Trouble

I don't know the exact moment I gave up on love, but I do remember the moment God said to me, "I cannot handle a bitter heart. I Am going to uproot everything that caused this."

The evening was in November 2017 just before Thanksgiving. I was at a live CD recording concert for a local artist and fellow church member. I had known about the concert, but I wasn't in the mood to attend because of the emotional massive attack I had suffered. The only thing I wanted to do that Saturday evening was drink a few glasses of wine and Netflix and chill by myself. It was what I had done for the most part to soothe the pain that was raging in my heart. To be honest, I'm surprised I didn't become an alcoholic from all the drinking I had done. Can somebody say, "BUT GOD" with me?

One of my dear friends, A.P., knew of the trauma and had pretty much forced my hand to attend. She wouldn't stop bringing it up and even offered to pick me up. After a week or so of saying, "I'll think about it," while knowing my thoughts were not to go, I had a change of heart, the first in a long time. It would be the night the double-edged sword of God would cut me to add to me and cut me to remove things that are not and were not of Him.

The way He began the much-needed surgery on my heart was very unexpected. During the concert, the train of God filled the room with His glory. Beyond the music, it was the authentic worship and praise that welcomed Him in. There was one part of the recording that I'll never forget, oddly enough, it was the only moment that remained in my memory bank.
Here's what happened…

I was standing next to my friend as we worshipped and loved on the Lord with all the other attendees. With my hands up in a surrendering position, I heard God say to me, "Remove your glasses." Now, when He says to remove my glasses and/or earrings, I know whatever follows afterward will send me into what is referred to as a Baptist fit. Every time He'd instructed me prior to that, I would take off running, dancing, and bucking around with a loud shout of praise to my Jesus. Knowing this, I did as He said.

After I placed my glasses in my purse, He then said, "I cannot handle a bitter heart. I Am going to remove everything that caused this." Hearing those words, I began to cry, but my crying didn't last long. Moments, and by moments I mean it had to be seconds, had passed before I heard a sound coming from the organ. It was a key that I hadn't heard before nor since that night. When the key was struck, I felt the Spirit of God fall on me. In being overcome with His presence, I felt a sting in my heart. It was a prink that I felt. I believe it was God beginning the repairing of my heart.

I don't know how long I was having a fit, but when I came down, the only thing I could say was, "Thank You, Lord." I repeated my thanks to Him because that was how I felt. I was thankful that help for me had finally arrived.

The arrival of the help I had asked for was quick to come, but the process, was not so much. It was a long, slow, soul and spirit-altering timeframe. I would be in surgery for almost two years. And because there was much to uproot, there was no anesthesia. I had to be aware of it all.

*****

In 2018, a friend sent me an email about feeling depressed and how that depression was taking over her life. This was my reply...

I know how you feel all too well. My heart knows where this can lead because I've been down this same path. Yet, the help I received was so unexpected. It came at a time when I really didn't care if I lived, died, or went to Heaven or hell. I figured death couldn't be so bad because I felt like every day I lived I was just slowly dying. I thought that hell couldn't be any worse because each day was hell for me, at least my version of hell.

There were days that blurred together, weeks that I had no track of time, months that seemed like years because I masked it with drinking, men, sex, and food. All those things filled a void in my life but because they were all temporary and held no valuable substance, my depression became worse. I was all alone in a crowded world.

I know what depression is, it's a feeling like you have no purpose in life, a wish that it all would end. Life can be too heavy and no one can understand. People say, "Run to God," but how could you—well, me at that time—run to a God I knew nothing about? It's like a random unknown person asking to borrow a few hundred dollars. You wouldn't do it because you have no relationship with the person. And if you did have a relationship with the person seeking the money, you would have to have some type of trust that you would be paid back. Well, that's how it was. I didn't know God, had no relationship with Him, and couldn't trust what I didn't know. But the last week in Dec 2011 I had this overwhelming feeling to attend church. It was on NYE night that I had an encounter with a Man that would change my life, give me a new direction, save me from a world that had no love for me, and would give me a new name and purpose. That Man was Jesus.

It was a long time coming and a journey I wouldn't want anyone to take.

Through the years, I learned who God is, how much He loves me (Isaiah 43:1-7), and just why I was born for a time such as this. I had to build a relationship with Him and as I did everything that was temporarily filling the voids in my life were removed and those voids became filled with the love and security I'd found in Christ. Some saints of the Lord will never admit to being depressed, but I'm not the saint that hides from where God has brought me from.

I haven't had one bout of depression since God snatched me up. I've been sad and upset but not depressed. I know you know God, but do you know Him intimately? Do you know Him to the point where you can think about Him and your whole day turns around, not to mention the turnaround in your life? Depression is a mind thing. But God declares, in Isaiah 26:3-4 "Thou wilt keep him in perfect peace, whose mind is stayed on thee: because he trusteth in thee. Trust ye in the Lord for ever: for in the Lord Jehovah is everlasting strength:"

Trust in the Lord and keep your mind on Him. The vices of this world are tricks of the enemy to keep you away from God and from fulfilling your destiny. You are loved, honored, and cherished. Seek the One you know of so you may know Him.

I pray, in the name of Jesus, that you receive healing of your mind and a lift in your spirit. The Word of God declares, in Philippians 2:10, "That at the NAME OF JESUS every knee should bow, of things in heaven, and things in earth, and things under the earth;"

Therefore, I pray with the authority of Christ. Everything has a name and depression is a name. That name has a knee that it must bow down and out of you. It has no place in you. I call it out, now. I send it back to where it came from so that the Spirit of the Lord can have His perfect way. I rebuke the taste of alcohol from your lips, tongue, and throat. May it be sour to the taste. I pray when you taste the Lord and see that He is good, you find that He is all that you desire to consume (Psalm 34:8, Taste and see that the Lord is good: blessed is the man that trusteth in Him.)

I pray that anyone seeking to keep you from progressing falls by the way side and are seen no more. In the name of Jesus, I pray to my, your, our Father that is in heaven. Amen.

The Restorer, The Mechanic, and the Crew

Tucked snuggly against a wall, with other junk cars in front of and behind it, was an end-of-life vehicle. The car, once one of the most sought after in its prior years, had seen better days.

The owner of the vehicle had called a salvage yard for it to be recycled for scraps. After receiving a few hundred dollars for it, the owner believed it was a simple process to get rid of it. The owner of the salvage yard to the seller, "We'll strip all identifying marks from it like the VIN number, which we'll have removed out of the DMV system. This means nobody can buy it or refurbish it and we can't sell it without the new buyer knowing it's a salvaged vehicle. We call these types end-of-life."
Never having heard the term before, the seller asked, "What does that mean?"

"It simply means it has reached the end of its use, most times from natural wear and tear, flooding, or a fire. Or in most cases, a bad accident. Looking at this one, it's been used up a lot." They shared a laugh as the owner agreed that it had, "Been in the family for over forty years. It was my dad's, then mine. I gave it to my son for his sixteenth birthday eight years ago. If I'm not mistaken, my dad got it from his childhood best friend's father some years back. We decided to give her a rest after the bottom of the driver's side rusted out badly and fell while my son was driving it."

"Is he okay?"

"Oh, yes. He's fine. It just freaked him out a bit. But he was able to control the steering wheel and come to a stop on the side of the road. He called me crying but was okay. He said, 'Dad, I'm done. I don't want this crap car anymore.' So, here we are."

"Well, this ol' girl has seen better days. We'll make sure to get the last bit of what's usable out of her."

"Good to know nothing of worth will be left behind."

"Yea, we take everything of value out of it. It's called depolluting. If we can repurpose it, sell it, or recycle it, we do. Basically, nothing that can harm the environment remains. We also can choose to sell it to steel factories and processors who then take it and melt it down for consumers' goods. The ol' girl will probably end up in another car in a year or so."

"Wow. All of that comes out of an old junk car? Fascinating stuff."

"Yea. A lot can come from an undrivable heap of metal. Everything from the precious metals, copper wiring, batteries, plastics, wheels, and more is good for something else, but not for use on this ol' girl."

After they ended the chat, the transaction, and then parted ways, the car was hauled off to its final destination. In a short while, it would no longer see paved roads, tall buildings, and tree-lined streets with well-manicured lawns that were the welcoming signs of flawlessly painted family homes. The last time that car was filled with gasoline was the last time it would be. A refreshing carwash made sure no bird poop, dust from pollen or splatted bugs stuck to it. It was going to a place of for sure death, never to be recognized for the good it had for so long. Every driver it ever had would become a faded, distant, unrecallable memory.

When the car arrived, it was lowered from the flatbed onto a weighing station. Coming in at just under six tons, it was then hitched to a pickup truck and maneuvered into the spot it would be kept until the time of demise arrived. A few days later, the junkyard owner had planned to crush it and prepared for further processing along with a few other junk cars that could make him a few thousand dollars once sold to a steel factory.

Making a list of the cars he wanted to break down, he saw that he had twelve on his list before he was interrupted in his count. A few yards away from the rusted car, a restorer of vintage cars come along to purchase it. The seller of the junk tried to get the restorer to see that although he can sell it to him, he didn't think it would be worth the time and investment of money to restore. "It's past the end of life. There's nothing more you can get out of it. I wouldn't want you to, you know, work hard on this crap just to bring it back to me in the end. Trust me, look for something else."

"I don't want to look for any other. I want this one. I saw it on your website for sale as is. I want it as it is. Name your price."

"Okay, buddy. You got it, it's your money."
Looking at the car, the restorer says, "You don't see what I see but it'll be worth it."

Buying the clunker, he had it loaded onto the back of a trailer hitch and gladly hauled his treasure away. Arriving at his home, he removed the car from the hitch and set it into a temperature-controlled garage. What the restorer knew was that he had to keep the car from rusting out even more and to do that the temperature needed to be steady.

Surveying what needed to be done to bring it back to its glory days, the restorer opened the car doors, popped the trunk and hood to take a closer look. He knew it would need a new engine and other new parts to make it run, but he wanted to see if it would start. Sliding into the front seat, he rubbed his hands over the genuine leather steering wheel and smiled.

"They don't make them like this anymore."
Taking the key, he inserted it and hoped that it started. Pressing the break, he held his breath as he turned the key in the ignition. At first, it didn't want to turn over. Then he remembered, "I need gas."

While it was being prepared at the salvage yard for depollution, the gas and all oils were removed. The restorer grabbed the oil and gas can and refilled each as much as he could. He tried, again, and that time it turned on, making a loud roaring sound. Removing his foot from the brake, he tried to shift the gear to see if it would move back or forward just a bit, not enough to take off down the road, just enough to see if it could be moved without a push. To his surprise, it did move forward. Shifting the car and feeling hopeful, he put it in reverse. After giving it a little gas, he was surprised yet again when it moved backward.

"Yes!" he said as he shifted it once more, this time into park.

Leaving the car on, he and his friend, a highly experienced mechanic, discussed what work needed to be done under the hood. They decided that nothing would be worth keeping and that replacement parts would be best to ensure proper restoration. They continued to inspect the car to determine what other items they'd need for their project. From paint color for the exterior to wood for the interior, along with the soft leather for the steering wheel, all details were decided on that day. The restorer was excited to get to work on his project, it was a dream of his to do so.

He had searched for that specific model and year for decades. Every time he was close to securing one, it would fall off the radar. Oftentimes he was out bided by someone else, but he never lost hope that he would get one. For years, he knew he could do something good with the junk yard car. There was no doubt in his mind that he could make it the best, if not better than it was before it landed in the junkyard.

The restorer and the mechanic proceed to order the necessary parts for the car. At the end of it all, it was determined that it would take just under two years to get everything that was needed. The restorer's only comment was, "It's worth it," as he looked over from his seat at the bar at which he and the mechanic sat. At the end of the day, the restorer closed the garage door, locked it and walked away until the week he would begin to work.

When he returned to the old, outdated vehicle, the same admiration he had when he first saw it, was the admiration he still had for it. He marveled at its rusted beauty. Putting on protective gear and gloves, he grabbed the tools needed to remove the doors, the hood, the trunk. As he began, the mechanic arrived with two helpers in tow. Together, the four of them dismantled the car, unscrewing bolts, pulling latches, and popping hard to remove pieces of metal. It took the crew roughly two hours to take it all apart, time that was well spent for the crew.

At the end of the demolition, the crew stood back as the restorer launched his vision for the car. They marveled at the new additions that would be applied to the restoration. Nodding their heads, taking notes, and being shown around the car as the vision was poured out, they were happy to be on board and the restorer was happy to have them on board.

Asking questions for clarity, the crew wrote the vision down and understood what part of it they would collectively and individually be responsible for. The team split off to dive into what they were going to take care of to bring the vision forward. The group drew up the plans for their respective tasks and finished the day ready for the next.

As time went on, packages were delivered, supplies purchased from local hardware stores, and new paint matched that of old. Before they knew it a year had passed by. Taking pictures and videos to remember the process, the restorer saved them as proof of the team's hard work and dedication.

"We're almost there," the mechanic said to the restorer.

"Yes, I see. I'm very proud of the handiwork." He stood back and wiped a tear that wanted to fall from the proudness in his heart.

"I'm proud too. We just need to wait for the parts on the engine. I'm hoping they'll get here in the next few weeks. I apologize that it's taking so long. The parts are being custom made just for this car."

"No need to apologize. I understand and am happy that the pieces will be custom made for this wonderful piece of work.

The time it takes doesn't worry me. It'll be worth the wait in the end."

With nothing else to do to the body and under the hood, the restorer ordered additional items to spruce up the car. He ordered new floormats for the interior and the trunk and special leather for the car seats and steering wheel. Adding to the beauty that was yet to behold, he purchased ebony wood grain for the console and the steering wheel.

Weeks later, the restorer contacted the mechanic and told him, "I just received a shipment of the final part for the engine. Let's get this car fired up again."

Agreeing and eager to get it done, the team gathered for teleconference and agreed to work on the car for the next two weeks straight to get the parts in for the engine. Finally, eight days later, ending sooner than expected, the restorer slid into the car and watched one of the crew members use a gas can to put premium plus gasoline into the tank. The restorer smoothed his hands across the soft butter leather, the wood of the inlay, and the softness of the velvet on the interior roof of the car.

The smell of the restored car was pleasing to his nostrils. Taking a deep breath, he let it out slowly and added, "This is as sweet as a rose."

He closed his eyes and leaned back into the comfort of the seat. Letting his head fall back on the headrest, he gripped the steering wheel, felt around for the ignition, and turned the key. The sound of the car staring sent chills through his body and caused the crew to roar in excitement. They hugged, gave handshakes, and slapped the car.

The restorer opened his eyes to see the crew that was with him from the start cheering and celebrating. He was honored to have them by his side for nearly two years. Their dedication to the project matched his. They even offered up solutions to issues that arose during the process.

Looking at them, he said, "Hey, guys, let's go for a spin. Quickly, they all piled in.

Someone yelled, "Let's go!"

Another added, "Let's burn some rubber!"
The restorer put the car in drive, pressed the gas, and eased out of the garage. The sun was bright in the sky that day.
The mechanic said, "Let's put the top down."
The restorer turned to him, "Sure. Go ahead."
Grinning from ear to ear, the mechanic pressed the button that would remove the top of the car. As the top lowered, the guys looked up at the folding velvet top.
From the back of the car the restorer heard, "Ooowww."
Once the top was down and folded into the hatch, he turned to look at the crew as the sun fell on them all.
     "We ready?" He asked them.
In unison, they all answered, "Yea!"

Allow the Potter to Work.

There will be times when you feel like people are achieving, arriving, and/or succeeding far more than you are. When you think you're close to the troubled waters, someone comes out of nowhere, knocking you down. After a long while, after long-suffering, you can feel defeated and give up. You have been stepped over, stepped on, or just kicked down. Plus, there's no one in sight to help you.

You can will to do what you wish to do, but you give up before you actually get started. Yet, there is a Man that hasn't stopped looking at you. He waited for the perfect time, during the troubling of the waters, to step in and give you the help you needed. He doesn't look down at those who are on the ground and think, "She didn't try hard enough to get where she wanted to go. So, why should I help?"

Woman of God, He sees you trying to do all that is within your power to go forth. He notices all the people going before you, people using you for their own gain. He sees how long it's been going on. Just when you think all is lost is when He'll step in and, without even sending you where you wanted to go, He'll give you a new direction that is far better than where you thought you needed to be. He's just that good.

Woman of God, worry not about who goes before you. They may be going the wrong way. The true Way is just steps from turning you around.

That day shall surely come.

Like the Restorer, The Mechanic, and the Crew

While writing this book, I had to remember what He said to keep me from falling deeper into a place that would take me years to recover from.

"Let Me be Who I Am."

"I love you because you are Mine. You are Mine because I love you."

"I Am your God, daughter."

"You are precious to Me."

Through the work of God's skillful hands, I had become someone new, someone I didn't know I could become. He was restoring me, reviving the parts of me that had died long ago.

I am the car. God is the Restorer. The mechanic is Jesus. The crew is the Holy Spirit. The tools are His Word and the people He used in my life for His glory.

Trusting God for the healing, repairing, and mending of my heart was easy to do. What was hardest was the aftereffect.

See, like the restored vintage car, I felt my heart had been through so much to get it to a healthy place that I couldn't see myself in a relationship anymore. I couldn't see myself giving my heart to a man just for him to break it. Still interested in men, I didn't want to risk the work that needed to be done. Fearing that someone would plant a seed of bitterness in my heart that would later blossom was too much for me to handle. Keeping to myself, I kept my head down and minded the work He gave me to do.

If a guy tried to talk to me to get to know me, I would look at him and say, "Nope. You're going to destroy me." Giving them a chance wasn't an option. It would be the first time that I used the "Friend Zone." Before the heart attack, I just allowed a guy to be whatever he wanted to be in my life. If he wanted to be friend, friends we would be. If he wanted to date me, dating we would be. If he just wanted sex, sex partners we would be. I didn't give myself the authority to dictate who would come into my life and what their position would be. I failed at seeing that I could control the aspect and that just because a man wanted me, didn't mean he was going to have me. It would be a year or so before I was able to apply the lesson I had learned and I must say, I did very well.

A guy "friended" me on Facebook and after about a week, asked me on a date. We had dinner which was accompanied by great conversation. At the end of the date, he asked me to go to the movies later that week and we did. After the movies, he came to my home. We watched another movie before I asked him to leave. I did so because, although I was comfortable with him being in my space, I heard the Restorer say, "He wants you". I immediately knew what "wants you" meant.

I told my date that I felt he needed to leave because I knew where this night was heading. Without disagreeing, he left. Closing and locking my front door, I yelled, thank you!" I was happy that He spoke to me and that He gave me what I needed to make a good decision and to not feel as if I couldn't.

After the second date with this man, I knew something wasn't right, something was off. Eventually, he ghosted me and to be honest, I'm glad he did. I could have asked him why he disappeared but didn't. I didn't have the need to know why. I'm glad I listened to discernment because six months later, he was married. Had I not paid attention, I would have been tangled up in some mess with a man that belonged to another woman.

I'm learning in this recovery phase that the more I pray, the wiser I become. Praying for discernment around a man's intentions is a huge deal for me. I listen out for God's words and moved accordingly thereafter. He hasn't let me down and never will. I know that men, just as I am, are flawed humans. Perfect we are not and never will be. My desire is just to be a wise imperfect person.

I think the way to gaining safety in a relationship is to first do so in Christ. This journey has forced me to focus on Him like never before. Remember as a kid when you would become hurt, how you ran to your mom or dad for comfort? Or a grandparent that you were close to? It didn't matter how much or how little the pain was, what mattered was that you were in it and wanted a kiss and a hug to make it feel better. That's how it is for me now. Whenever I feel a hint of pain from anything, I run to my Father. Holding back how I feel is no longer an option. I want Him to know the matters of my heart because it is through Him that the pain will be healed. I know I couldn't or can't heal me on my own, which I why I expect Him to do it.

Just like the vintage car, tucked away in the junkyard moments away from being changed forever until the restorer came along with an eye for beauty and saw the best in it, God saw and did the same for me. The restorer knew it was something to behold if the car could just be given a new life. God saw something in me that I didn't see in myself. He saw me whole, repaired, restored, healed, and at peace. Looking back, had I seen what was to come, I would have been more selective in those I allowed in my life. But I'm glad they came along and changed me, that change gave God the prime opportunity to show Himself as the healer and potter that He is.

The crazy part about being healed is the fear of being hurt again that comes with it. It's as if you know your heart and soul are in a good place and the last thing you want is for someone to disrupt the peace that came from God. Yet, the desire for a husband and family of your own hasn't gone away.

I remember praying for God to remove my fear of falling in love for real this time. I asked Him to allow me the ability to give grace to a deserving man for real this time. Being the kind God that He is, He gave me the peace I needed to want to date again, for real this time, the peace to prepare me to date again, for real this time. He changed my heart toward the type of men I'd been attracted to before the heart attack so that when I do love, it will be for real this time!

His Vision and His Vision

The funny thing about a heart attack is that what used to be attractive and attracted to you, no longer is.
I used to like a particular type of man. One that wasn't where he wanted to be but had the potential. I thought that with my guidance and influence, I could help him become a better man. I was sure, without a doubt, that if I poured everything that I had into him, then when it came time to choose a "wife for life," and the "mother of my children," then I would be chosen. I would be the one he'd see was always there in his deepest struggle. I hoped that I would be the one he thought of when he looked at the future ahead. Nothing prepared me for the rejection I would receive when I wasn't the one on his arm.

I remember doing this "service," to a guy named Walter. When he had reached a place of peace in Jesus, which is what he said, I was sure that he would finally see me and want to date me. Nope! That didn't happen. Instead of moving into the future with me, he moved back to his past and proceeded to move forward with her. Sadly, I learned that when dating, potential doesn't mean a thing. We all have potential, but it's the reality of what we do or don't do that can turn our potential into something that is tangible.

Since the recovery, my desire for men is far different. I desire a man that is actively in his purpose, one that doesn't need me to build him to his potential, but to support him as he does it. I desire a man that knows where he is going in life, has a plan, is secure in himself, and wants all that God says is his. My hope is to make a specific petition to God: "Lord, he shared with me the vision for his life, please show me what I am responsible for. Build me now for what I have to carry later. Give me the wisdom now that will be required, later. Show me the path that I am to walk to be his help meet now to ensure I arrive on time. This is my praying wife's prayer. In Jesus' name. Amen."

I truly can't wait to send that up to God. I can't wait to be in His presence and pray for my husband's vision and the parts of it that I'm to handle. Like, if God said his vision goes from A-Z and the parts I am responsible for are at E, M, J, T and W, you better believe I'll be in prep mode. It may sound like it's being a bit "extra" for a wife, but I believe that my husband is deserving of a wife that is in sync with his vision and His vision. Whether or not my husband sees me as what he needs to accomplish his vision, God knows that I'll be in position at the right time to be the help meet that I am.

Will he be perfect?

Not even close!

He doesn't have to be close to perfection, just perfect in his passion for the things in life. That passion will drive him to his purpose and destiny.

Allowing God to do a good thing in you is better than you are thinking you can do it alone. I tried. It doesn't work. He is the Mechanic. He knows how to repair what was broken. At times, all the missing pieces don't make it back into the redesign. He does something new, gives you a new look on life, a Godly perspective in exchange for a worldly one.

As I write this manuscript, I'm reminded of all the work He has done to repair the damage that was done. At times I cry, wondering why I allowed, accepted, or didn't stop the ill treatment toward me. While holding myself accountable for my own actions, I was also reminded of how I had to take responsibility for my part in those relationship failures. As hard as it was, I was able to see my own imperfections, faults, failures and flaws.

But God...
God really does want you. He really does want to heal you, restore you, and bring you back to a better place than the one you were in before and the one you're in now.

After All, They Still Don't Know You.

Woman of God,

By now you've run into old friends, love interests, and family members that were around during your B.C. (before Christ) days. They reminisce on the things you used to do, the attitude you use to have, the lifestyle you proudly flaunted. Some consistently remind you of your *heyday*. I know it can become bothersome at times, but try not to let it vex you, upset you, or change your mood.

See, they can't see you *now* if they've never taken a step with you. They've stepped with you in the club, at the party, or stepped to you for a date. But have they stepped with you in Christ? If they had, they'd be less likely to bring up what is covered by the blood of Jesus. There will be those that will only see your past, they'll never want to see what God has done and is doing with you. It's not you, darling, it's them! You're free from the title of "Party Girl" because you're now the #DaughterOfAKing. You've been adopted into a royal priesthood. Your sins have been covered by love and are no longer seen by God. Stand firm and continue to let God do a good thing in you.

(1 Peter 2:9; 1 Peter 4:8; Isa 43:25; Gal 1:13-15, 22)

Processing the Pain

The process to get from a junky heart to a beautiful one was almost two years. I was forced to face my own demons, demons that had plagued my life for over twenty years. The sex and pornography addictions were the first to be removed by the Restorer.

I had to handle the fear of rejection and the feeling unworthiness. I didn't think, for a long time, that I was loveable or that I could be someone's wife and mother to his children. It wasn't that I didn't think it wasn't possible for me, I just didn't think I could because of all the prior relationships. I was always wondering, "Why not me?" when either of them would move on from me, have children, get married or be in a long-committed relationship. I felt I wasn't enough. Feeling that way was normal for me, but during the recovery, I learned that I was and am enough. I just tried really hard to put myself in the hands of men that couldn't hold me.

My mentor, Vanessa, told me that I was enough, I've always been such. The men that I tried to put myself in the hands of didn't have hands big enough to hold me. Those words, planted at the right time, would dwell in my mind for years to follow. It was the new seed that my heart needed but hadn't yet received. I believed I was enough, but feeling it wasn't the same. Processing the pain of the past stopped me from connecting what I believed to what I felt. My feelings let me down so much that I didn't want my heart to believe in what I couldn't confirm. Well, to get my confirmation, I ended up fasting over the course of three-days. It wasn't planned, it just happened.

During the fast, I asked God if I was enough for Him. I didn't get a response until the last day of the fast. He, again, was so kind to me. I remember hearing, "Daughter, you have always been enough. I have made with all that you will need for the one I Am preparing for you. He will not let you fall as others in your past have. If you allow Me to work, you will see My glory in your life and in his."

Changing my mind had to happen through a change of heart. It didn't matter how much my mind wanted to believe, if my heart felt something different, then it would change my mind to what it felt. That's why I follow my heart instead of my head. My heart is where my treasures are stored up. I can't allow anyone into it.

Having God in place as my guard has kept me from falling over into territory that would or could destroy me. Like the vintage car, it had taken a lot of tearing down, a lot of ordering premium pieces, many tools that could handle the work, and an eye for beauty seen through the restorer. It was the old parts that no longer functioned as they were designed to due to the wear and tear that really had the restorer and his crew working hard.

The base of the floor rusting and falling out was as my hope in love towards and from man. The smooth leather steering wheel was the last of the love I had remaining. I used to tell God, "I don't have much more to give. I have enough love in my Bank of Love for one more withdrawal. After that, I'll be in the negative." I don't recall what He said to my comment, but I do know that like the car, He put the fuel in me that gave me the drive to keep going.

Waiting for Him to complete His work on me was also a test of my patience. I was over having old relationships resurface. It was random remembrances that were triggered by a word I heard in church every single time I remembered. I can't tell you how many times I found myself at the altar of the church having the old parts pulled out just to walk away with faded memories.

If you can imagine a stripped-down car, nothing but the frame sitting on bricks. No doors. No windows. No brakes. No bumpers. No engine. No seats. No lights. No hood or trunk door. Just a shell of what used to be. Looking at it, you can tell it was a car. The age of it and the brand may be clear if you're well versed in cars, but anything of what it looked like in the past is gone. The steering wheel and some of the electronics remain but aren't useable since what kept it going s missing. The heart of it, the engine.

Brokenness before God is a good thing. I know it doesn't seem like it, but it is.

The Lord is near to the brokenhearted and saves those who are crushed in spirit.
Psalm 34:18 NKJV

He can look and see where you try to hide, cover up, push under the rug the things that matter to your heart. With love and kindness does He draw it out so that you can be free to love Him. See, what I've learned through this process is how my jacked-up heart caused me to be on reserve about getting close to Him. I would come to Him just enough for me to feel safe in doing so, but when I had to become vulnerable to God, I would back up. For me, this looked like me believing in what He said about the lives of others, but I was hard pressed to believe about my own.

If you told me God said something specifically about your life, without doubt, hesitation, or fear I believed for you. I prayed with you, fasted if needed and kept you encouraged until you saw what He said. But for myself, it would take some time before I trusted what I heard, let alone believed it. I would be hesitant to pray about it because I wasn't sure if I heard what I had. I didn't want God to tell me that He hadn't said what I thought He said. I was afraid to trust Him on behalf of my own life.

The areas in which I lacked trust were in the relationship department. Those years were dreadful for me. My head was filled with thoughts of what if's. What if at this late age it becomes hard to be found? I go out for fun with my family, my friends, and by myself, but no one is asking me out. What if a man wants to take a few years to get married and more before he's ready for children? How old will I be then? What if I didn't hear Him like I thought? Then what was it that I actually heard? What if it's too late for me to have children? I'm on the wrong side of thirty-five. I'm considered high-risk now. What if my body can't support a child until full term? I had one miscarriage at nineteen and pregnancy never happened thereafter.

Those times I had to fight through the what ifs made me stronger at times and weak at others. However, it was He who remained consistent in His love for me. He showed me He was worthy of my trust, my complete, unfiltered, and unwavering trust.

The point of processing the pain is sitting with what hurts and determining where it's coming from. In those times, in those spaces, the King of Glory will reveal, heal, and change your mind and heart. At the end of that fast, I had processed the pain to the point where I, again, felt ready to date. I was no longer afraid of what man could do to me because God was/is with me. I began to feel and believe that I am enough for not just any man but for one man. And he will, too, be enough for me.

Stripped Down to Nothing

Like an old car that needs to be prepped for restoration, everything I thought I knew about myself, about love, and about relationships had to be removed.

The first thing God did was remove the hood, which in this case was the blinders to life I had on. I was looking through tinted, rose-colored glasses my entire life. Everything was beautiful. I saw no fault in people, myself, or anything that mattered to me. I was always seeing life's cup as half full with room to add more. However, it wasn't in my best interest to see things that way. I had to see life the way that it was. Seeing people for who they were made me not only look for the good, but for the truth, for ill intentions, for deceitful natures and for hidden agendas. The breaker to it all was when He showed me myself first.

For a long while I used to think it was the men's fault that led to our breakups. I only spoke about their downfalls, their cheating, their lack of communication, their fake love, and their affection for me or their lack thereof. I wouldn't share what my toxic behaviors were and how they played a part in everything. Oh no. I wanted to play the victim, to win the Oscar, and to star in the next movie.

When God showed me myself in each relationship, I had no choice but to take accountability for my actions or the lack thereof. I had to acknowledge that I wasn't a victim in it, but a co-star to their actions or to lack thereof. It all went hand-in hand. Here's what I learned about me as God stripped me down to nothing so that I could see everything.

The tendency to think I deserved more than what I gave. In my heart, I knew I didn't love them the way they deserved to be loved. I had my own hidden agenda, which, if you didn't know, was to have a child. I was clear to only believe in what I wanted to instead of acknowledging truth of why I wanted them in the first place. I would say that I never had a chance to love a man the way I wanted to, but the real reason I never could was because I didn't love me for me. I had, as I said before, a strong like of myself, but not love.

How could I ask for something I couldn't give myself? I don't know, but I do know that I love me now. Getting to a place of self-love has helped me to make better decisions beyond the love and relationship areas of life. From the friends I choose to the way I spend my time, the foods I consume to the way I protect my eye and ear gates all costs, it all comes back to loving myself. Being able to tell someone how their actions affect me without holding back is me loving me.

Attempting to force a relationship where one wasn't requested. I know what it's like to want someone to want you. I know what it's like when they reject you for their own reasons. That rejection creates hurt and fear inside. For some, even hate can become a side effect of rejection. Putting myself in harm's way wasn't something I liked to do. Harm's way for me was trying to do everything I thought a guy would like just for him to see me. I wanted him to see me for who I was. I wanted him to see the possibilities of life, family, love and a relationship with me.

To accomplish my goals, I would learn what a man's needs were and where there was a lack I would fill it. Before I was a saved woman, I would be a filler for a man's pockets, for his drug habits, for his party expenses, and for whatever else he needed. I did whatever I needed to do to make me seem valuable and so as not to be overlooked. I wanted to be the top option for a man when he was looking for a wife. I thought for sure that if I did those things, the things he needed that I would surely be chosen and made into a wife.

Then, once I became saved, my tactics changed a bit. When I was interested in a man, I would search for his weaknesses in his faith journey with God and play on them. I can't believe I'm admitting this right now, but being a follower of Jesus, how could I be so manipulative toward His people?
Easy.
I just had done it.

I wanted to spin their hearts, not so they would go God but so they would come to me. I wanted them to see me in the midst of their problems, issues, troubles and trials instead of God. I felt like if and when they finally emerged from the dark place, they would see it was me in there with them. Not God. I was trying my hardest for them to see that the wife in me was ready for the husband in them. Again, I was wrong. Sitting in my office crafting this book, I 'm not proud of the woman I use to be. I am, however, proud of the woman I am today. I guess it was Gods' hand on my life and theirs to keep them from falling for my traps.

Ignoring my fly red flags. When I didn't get my way, I ended the relationships. Honestly, I could have stayed in many of them. The relationship with William and John could have been saved. The others, not so much. I know now as I'm reflecting on the times I had with those two in particular, that had I just gotten on their agendas instead of trying to get them on my mine, we would have been where I desired. Or so I believe.

Because they were the last hopes I had before and after Christ, respectfully, I think that I was pushing too fast instead of enjoying what we had. I didn't want to accept what they were giving me because it wasn't what I wanted, but I did feel, at those times of ending the relationships, that my needs weren't being met. To be clear, if it wasn't already so, I didn't know what my needs were. I had no idea what it meant to have a man that I needed as opposed to just wanting. I wanted them for my own selfish reasons and nothing more.

I used to ask myself what I needed in a man, in a husband, and when I answered, it was all superficial. He had to be tall, with his own car, house/apartment, no kids, no bad debt, no bad health issues, love to travel and more. They were things. Things. Things that I needed him to have. I wasn't concerned with the need of a man with integrity, loyalty, a healthy mind and a relationship with Christ. My needs weren't established which led to me wanting from the men whatever I wanted instead of what I needed.

The more God removed of me, the more of me was revealed. Along with that were the realizations that I had missed out on so many things that a healthy relationship could bring. Once God removed the engine of the old, rusted car, my overall desires became clear.

I wanted to be loved. Although I hadn't loved me and yet wanted to be loved, I didn't really know what that would feel like. I thought being loved from me was to have sex with a man and from him was to make me feel special. Since the love I was used to giving and receiving was very shallow, when an issue arose between us, I was easily bothered and would easily end the relationship. Because my love was very superficial, I had no reason to remain. I had no fight in me, only flight. And that was what I did. Very well. It wasn't until God stopped me in my tracks with His love that I had to fight to know what love really was and how it felt for me. Allowing God to show me changed my perspective of love from a man, but more importantly, for myself. Loving me wasn't an easy thing to do. I had to first see that I was worthy of it and that nothing but my thoughts caused me to miss it. I had to change my mind about myself. I had to stop replaying all the things I'd heard from others concerning me.

Then there was forgiveness. I had to forgive me for what I allowed to happen, for what happened without my consent, and for what I did to myself. I had to forgive the men that I would never ask for it and I had to ask them to forgive me. Although, I hadn't seen or heard from either of them, except John, I still had to ask. When it comes to forgiveness, God taught me that I not only had to ask for it, but receive it. I'd asked God to forgive me of deeds I had done. When He did, I still felt bad about those deeds. I kept apologizing for what I'd done even after He'd forgot about it (I, I am he who blots out your transgressions for my own sake, and I will not remember your sins. Isaiah 43:25 ESV). I couldn't let it go although He did.

What He said to me one day, changed my life in such a simple way. "Daughter," He said sweetly as I prepared to meet up with a few friends. There was comfort in His voice and it gave me much more when He said, "You are forgiven. You have to receive your forgiveness."

Receive.

Forgiveness.

I didn't know that asking for it was one thing, but honestly receiving it from Him was another.

I simply said, "Father, thank You for forgiving me. I receive it today."

I swear, as soon as I uttered those words, the weight of it all fell off of my shoulders. This was love for me. He showed me His love by forgiving me and teaching me how to receive it with His kindness. Showing me how to love me kept me from searching for it in man. I've learned that whatever I am seeking, it is in Him that I will find it.

Something as simple as flowers on a random day. Now, I know it doesn't seem like much to many, but flowers that arrive or are given just because mean much more than those received to celebrate something.

There was one time I was dating a guy when I was sixteen. We were driving around in his car one evening listening to music and talking. As we were, we stopped for a red light and there happened to be a man selling roses nearby. The guy I was dating got me two of them. It was the first and only time I had ever received flowers from a man. The only time. I tried to keep those rose alive forever. The other times were from my mom twice for my birthday, my co-workers who did so for my birthday, and from my mentor who had done so when I graduated with my associates degree in biblical studies. Those five times were the only times I had ever received flowers.

I used to feel bad when I thought about that. I wondered why I wasn't the type of woman a guy would want to buy flowers for. I wondered if I was deserving of such affection. What helped me overcome the sorrow that my heart felt from such a simple and meaningful act, was the day a co-worker of mine received flowers from her husband for no reason other than that he was showing his love to her. The flowers were bountiful and beautiful. I went to her desk and smiled and told her to tell her husband he's doing a great job loving on her. Later that day, another co-work mentioned that she wanted her boyfriend to send her flowers too. The next afternoon, that same co-worker received flowers from her boyfriend. I thought it too was a sweet gesture of love from him to her until she said she told him to send her flowers to the office.

For a moment, I was stuck on the asking part because it wasn't something he wanted to do for her. If it were, she wouldn't have had to ask. Then I became a bit confused. On one hand, if I don't tell a man that I would like him to send or give me flowers, how would he know? On the other hand, wouldn't a man know that a woman would appreciate the show of love?

While I tossed that flower ball around in my head, God slapped it to the ground. "You will not have to ask him to send or give you flowers. He will know because you are deserving of it." Not receiving flowers from a man that I was in a relationship hasn't bothered me since.

A Trip Around the World. As much as I love to travel, I've never had the pleasure of doing so with my man. Ever. Not even a ride to a nearby city. A baecation hasn't happened yet. This, too, I know may not mean much to others, but for me, it does. I believe that traveling can be stressful. I've traveled with one other person and in groups. The patience it takes to compromise on the planning of where to go, of where to stay and of what do, and dealing with all the other arrangements can put relationships to the test.

I believe that if a man and I can make it through a weekend away together that we can make it through something else. I haven't had the opportunity to do it yet, but I'm glad I haven't. I learned, through the guidance of my mentor, that not experiencing certain things with other men is a good thing. It means that what I do with my husband will have been shared with no other man but my husband. He'll be the only that can claim those memories with me. The memories he and I make can't and won't be compared to any other.

After all the work God did to strip me down to the bareness of myself, I was left with only who God said I was.

Chosen

Loved

Honored

Protected

Provision made

When He began to restore me, the things I wish I had done and experienced no longer mattered to me. I was giving God the opportunity to prove to me that I was and am worthy of what I desire.

The Turn Around at Midnight

Woman,

After everything I've experienced in my life— the good, the bad, the traumatic—here's what I know about God and His faithfulness: It Never Fails! There's a saying in church that goes, "Late in the midnight hour God is going to turn it around." It's one of those encouragement "quotes" that we say to help us and others through a problem/issue. But do you really believe He can and will turn things around for you?

For Israel, after God gave them precise instructions, they witnessed God turn their shackles into gold bracelets, a few cattle into many, and bondage into freedom (Exodus 12:35-38). While they minded His business, He minded theirs. In the middle of the night, He caused devastation to those that were an enemy of His chosen people. When Israel rose that next day, they were in a place of peace.

We are His chosen children. Whatever your problem is or whatever it is that keeps you from getting a good night's sleep, ask God to do something on your behalf in the middle of the night. You might have to pray during those precious hours or even fast—eating only what He says—to witness His glory.

Now, I don't know when your "turn around in the midnight hour" will come. Just be faithful in believing that it will arrive. And the next time you hear someone say or sing, "Late in the midnight hour God is going to turn it around," believe it. This "it" shall surely come to pass. In the midnight hour.

171

About the Author

Ebony Nicole Smith is a writing coach, publishing engineer, and published author. She has written several novels, devotionals, journals, and workbooks. Using her love for words as a guide, she has transformed her love into a passion to create stories that inspire, entertain, and nurture personal growth. With 20+ titles waiting to be written, Ebony Nicole will be busy for years to come.

Connect with Ebony Nicole

Facebook.com/coachebonynicole

Instagram.com/coachebonyniocle

Website: ebonynicolesmith.com

Email: info@ebonynicolesmith.com

Made in the USA
Middletown, DE
10 November 2022

14541973R00104